MEL BAY'S COMPLETE IRISH FIDDLE PLAYER

By Peter Cooper

A recording of the music in this book is now available. The publisher strongly recommends the use of this recording along with the text to insure accuracy of interpretation and ease in learning.

CONTENTS

PREFACE

Before writing this preface I picked up my fiddle and played a reel I was learning the day before. My version is still quite basic but the satisfaction I feel as it takes shape is one that other players, I am sure, will recognise. It is the enjoyment of recreating a traditional tune, of making it your own. This pleasure doesn't come without work. The art of the Irish fiddler is highly developed and can make considerable demands on the musician. It requires both technique and inventiveness. So don't expect to take up your fiddle and play like Michael Coleman or Tommy Peoples out of sheer enthusiasm, however naturally talented you may be! But you *can* expect to enjoy the process of learning.

This course is not for the total beginner on violin. You will need to be able to hold the fiddle and bow and play at least simple pieces in first position. Music-reading ability is also useful. All the tunes are recorded - note for note, as written - on the Learning Discs, but reading will enable you to follow the bowing, which is important. No experience of classical violin is needed, but anyone who has reached Grade 2 (Royal Irish Academy of Music or the Associated Board) or its equivalent should have no problem making a start here. It is important, of course, to listen to as much authentic traditional playing as possible. That, and working through *The Complete Irish Fiddle Player,* will give you a good practical grounding in style and technique.

My approach is based on the experience of teaching groups and individual students, young and old, over the past ten years or so. We learn bowing patterns and left-hand techniques as part and parcel of the tunes, so, while building up a repertoire, you are also developing a practical grasp of all the elements that make up the playing style. On the subject of repertoire, it has been estimated that there are over 6,000 Irish dance tunes currently in circulation! Some, however, are more common than others, so, although I've included a handful of rarities, most of the 80 tunes in this book are often played in sessions both in Ireland and throughout the Irish diaspora.

Acknowledgements

The titles of fiddle tunes are in reality just identification tags but I have used them as hooks on which to hang various bits of history, anecdote, folklore and literature. Thanks to all those who have given me photographs, stories and other information. This would have been a much drier book without their contributions.

The quotations from both Nell McCafferty and Maeve Binchy are from *Irish Life and Traditions*, edited by Sharon Gmelch, and are reproduced by courtesy of The O'Brien Press. The quotation from *Sentimental Education* by Gustave Flaubert, translated by Robert Baldick (Penguin Classics, 1964, page 83) is reproduced by permission of Penguin Books Ltd. Thanks to Mercier Press for permission to quote from Brendan Breathnach's *Folk Music and Dances of Ireland,* Eric Cross's *The Tailor And Ansty* and Mary Carbery's

The Farm By Lough Gur, the latter also by courtesy of Longman's. The quotations from *Brendan Behan's Ireland: An Irish Sketchbook* by Brendan Behan and Paul Hogarth and *The Scarperer* by Brendan Behan are reproduced by kind permission of Hutchinson and the Estate of the author. The quotation from Dr C.R.Halski's *Folk Music In Poland* is reproduced by permission of the author, as are the various quotations from Alan Ward's *Music From Sliabh Luachra*. Packie Manus Byrne, Steve Jones and publisher Roger Millington kindly let me use several extracts from Packie's *Recollections of a Donegal Man,* while Harry Bradshaw allowed me to quote from his Viva Voce booklet, *Michael Coleman 1891-1945* and from his notes to *James Morrison, The Professor.* Thank you to the Viking Press for the quotation from Maurice O'Sullivan's *Twenty Years A-Growing*.

Warmest thanks to all the traditional musicians, individually credited in the book or not, who have given me tunes; to Jane O'Connor for her inspiring violin tuition; to Bob Winquist and Joe Crane for reading the first draft; to Lawrie Wright and my sister Gillian Cooper for help with some of the chords; to Bill Whelan for invaluable assistance over in Dublin; and to all my fiddle students, past and present, without whom this book would certainly not have been possible. Finally I'd like to express my gratitude to Dr Coline Covington for her support and insight; to my partner Tricia Bickerton for her constant encouragement throughout the long process of putting the book together; and to my parents, Don and Avis Cooper - not least for paying for all my violin lessons as a youngster!

About the author

Born in the country near Stafford, England in 1951, Peter started violin at the age of nine and went on to study English at Balliol College, Oxford. In 1978 he became a professional fiddle player and singer, performing in Britain, Europe and the USA, first in partnership with Appalachian dulcimer player Holly Tannen (*Frosty Morning,*1979), then with traditional singer Peta Webb (*The Heart Is True,* 1986). Since the mid1980s Peter has concentrated on the study and teaching of folk fiddle styles. His first solo album, *All Around The World* (1990), released on his own *Fiddling From Scratch* label, featured music from Ireland, Scandinavia, Eastern Europe & the USA. His 1993 album, *The Wounded Hussar* explores the rich diversity of the Irish tradition and includes many of the tunes in this book.

Living in Hackney, London with his partner, Peter teaches on residential courses, runs adult education classes and gives individual tuition. He reviews for *Musical Traditions* and *Folk Roots* magazines and has composed music for films by Peter Greenaway and Moira Sweeney. As well as solo gigs, he performs as a member of Vivando, with Kathryn Locke and Geoff Coombs. Their first album, *Vivando,* released in 1995, includes some of his own compositions.

Address for correspondence: 86 Eleanor Road, Hackney, London E8 1DN,
England.

Peter Cooper

Photo: Ivan Coleman, 1994

Andy O'Boyle in a Camden Town pub, London, 1963 *Photo: Brian Shuel*

INTRODUCTION

'They were hard times and they were difficult times, but there was plenty of fun. There were weddings and wakes and all sorts of amusements that the people made themselves. The people were very interested in dancing in those days, and there were dancing masters...'
- Eric Cross, *The Tailor And Ansty*

What is traditional music?

Irish traditional music consists of the many songs and dance-tunes that have been passed on - more by example than formal teaching - from one singer or musician to another, often over generations and usually within families or communities. It's the dance tunes, of course, that I'm going to concentrate on. Once a tune has been accepted into the tradition a process of gradual change begins. Consciously or not, players will modify it according to their own taste, skill and limitations. The composer is forgotten - names in tune titles often refer to the person the tune was learned from - but the tune evolves. It's like the old story of the command passed along a column of marching soldiers: "Send reinforcements, we're going to advance!" By the time the last soldier delivers it, the message has become: "Send three-and-fourpence, we're going to a dance!" The Irish music we have today is very rich in variants and in this book, precisely because there is no one 'correct' version, different ways of playing the same phrase are given for many of the tunes.

A very brief history

The bulk of the dance music played today dates back to the 18th and 19th centuries. Foreign visitors to Ireland had long remarked on the people's insatiable appetite for dancing. Professional itinerant dancing masters catered to this demand, inventing and developing the steps for jigs, reels and hornpipes - still today the most important dance forms. The fiddle, from its first appearance across Europe in the 17th century, played a central part in this dance culture. Fiddlers, pipers and flute-players composed tunes in their thousands, often also adapting existing melodies to suit new dances, such as the sets of quadrilles which became fashionable in the 19th century.

Despite the relative depopulation of the Irish countryside during and after the Great Famine (1846-1851), 'crossroads' dances, held in the open air, remained common in summer, while in wintertime music took place in farmhouse kitchens - often sparsely furnished and, with their flagstone floors, ideal for dancing. 'American wakes', held when a member of the community was forced to emigrate, were other musical occasions that continued to occur well into the 20th century. This 'fireside' context gave the music a human, informal character, part of a social continuum of storytelling, gossip, card-playing, singing, matchmaking and so on that today might be referred to as the *craic*.

The Catholic clergy, however, saw such gatherings as sinful and frequently intervened to break them up. (See note on *The Musical Priest* - page 96). In 1935 the Public Dance Halls Act, brought in under pressure from the church and the police, finally made unlicensed dancing illegal. It is a strange irony that an independent Irish legislature should have suppressed the very culture which nationalist groups like the Gaelic League had sought in their struggle against British rule to promote.

Public dances were now held in parochial halls, with paid admission and under the watchful eye of the clergy. Professional or semi-pro groups, which came to be known as ceilidh (pronounced *kay-lee*) bands, played the dance-halls, sometimes adding drums, piano, even saxophone to the traditional instruments. Their performance may have sounded brash and heartless to ears accustomed to the older style of playing. But groups like the *Ballinakill Ceilidh Band* and the *Kilfenora Ceilidh Band* did a great deal to keep the music alive, while pulling in the dancers in great numbers. Throughout the 1940s and '50s ceilidh bands played a significant part in the increasingly urban lifestyle of the Irish in Britain and America, as well as back home in Ireland.

Irish emigration to the United States had led to the growth of Irish music enclaves in Boston, Philadelphia, New York and Chicago, which were to influence developments in Ireland. Francis O'Neill (1849-1936), chief of the Chicago police, collected dance tunes and airs during the last two decades of the 19th century and his *Music of Ireland,* first published in 1903 and later re-edited in various editions, helped establish or consolidate a common repertoire. O'Neill fought against the widespread indifference to Ireland's musical heritage, documenting, for example, the lives of Irish musicians of the time; and several of his descriptions are quoted in this book. Also influential, from the 1920s on, were the superb 78 rpm records which Irish fiddle players - and specifically, for some reason, players from County Sligo - recorded in America. Returning emigrants took the music of early recording stars like Michael Coleman back to Ireland.

Nevertheless, by mid-century the music scene back home was in poor shape, with emigration continuing to drain the countryside of young people. Even the records from America were a mixed blessing. Some players were undoubtedly inspired, but as many others may have been discouraged by the lack of recognition for their own efforts, especially if their local style lacked the obvious brilliance of the Sligo masters. By the 1940s, apart from the ceilidh bands, there was little or no public outlet for the music and, at grassroots level, it appeared to be in terminal decline.

Gradually, however, from the 1950s onwards that decline began to be reversed. Musicians themselves began forming clubs and organisations to promote traditional music, notably in 1951 the *Comhaltas Ceoltoiri Eireann* (The Irish Music Society), which within two years had set up the first annual *Fleadh Ceol* or music festival. Later in the 1950s radio broadcasts by music collectors like Ciaran Mac Mathuna and Seamus Ennis put fresh heart into the emergent revival scene and introduced traditional music to a new, young - and again increasingly urban - audience. Then in the 1960s and '70s, partly inspired by the folk boom in America, a veritable explosion of interest in Irish music took place.

Moving Cloud, a modern-day ceilidh band. Left to right: Maeve Donnelly, Carl Hession, Christy Dunne, Manus Maguire, Annette Stapleton and Paul Brock. Courtesy of Chris Sadler/Moving Cloud

The Chieftains, with fiddle players Sean Keane & Martin Fay Photo courtesy Claddagh Records Limited

At first it was the ballad-singing of groups like *The Clancy Brothers* and *The Dubliners* that came to the fore. And in Ireland it is usually their type of material - along with the songs of people like Bob Dylan - that is referred to by the term 'folk' music. But a big change occurred in the whole presentation of what - to distinguish it - is called 'traditional' music with the emergence of composer and arranger Sean O'Riada. Rejecting the ceilidh-band approach, he set fiddle, flute, uilleann (pronounced *ill-yun*) pipes and concertina alongside instruments more usually associated with baroque music, the harp and harpsichord. The drum-kit of the ceilidh band was replaced by the bodhran (pronounced *bow-rawn*), a shallow one-sided Irish drum. The new sound caught the imagination of public and critics alike and out of O'Riada's original group, *Ceoltoiri Chualann,* there emerged in 1963 what has probably been the most successful Irish band of subsequent decades, *The Chieftains.*

Other great bands followed in the 1970s, among them *De Danann* - featuring fiddler Frankie Gavin -, *The Bothy Band* - featuring fiddler Tommy Peoples - and *Planxty*, all combining a superb command of the traditional idiom with rock-music energy and presentation. They made a phenomenal impact internationally as well as at home, a revelation of what this music could be. I was one among the many whose passion for Irish music was ignited at this time. In the 1980s and 90's traditional Irish music has continued from strength to strength, with bands like *Moving Hearts, The Davy Spillane Band, Clannad, Stockton's Wing, Altan* and *Sharon Shannon* making it a major force in world music. Perhaps the best of it is that the success of the big-name bands and artistes has regenerated the music at grassroots level... But enough of this! Before we get dazzled with the glamour of it all, let's get down to some of the hard practicalities of actually *playing* the music!

Playing by heart

Whatever they play - whistle, flute, concertina, uilleann pipes, accordeon, mandolin, bodhran, mouth-organ or fiddle - traditional musicians play by heart. When they meet for a session no-one gets out a music stand and a tune-book. If they did, of course, the tunes would be more fixed than they are. In fact most players also <u>learn</u> their tunes by ear. Some would-be fiddlers, perhaps with a classical background, find this daunting but, if you are among them, don't worry. Learning by ear and playing by heart are skills that, like any other, can be acquired with practice. Familiarity with the idiom of Irish music makes it easier to learn a tune - though growing up with it from childhood is obviously best of all. Fiddle player Lucy Farr described to me her father's farm in County Galway in the 1920s :

> Every Friday night people gathered in the house and whatever instrument they had they brought with them. They played all night long. And as children we listened - because in those days children were seen and not heard. You just kept quiet but you learned the music. You had it - not pushed into you, but you couldn't help but learn it.

Barney Harrington, London 1970
Photo: John Harrison

Lucy Farr
Photo: courtesy of Lucy Farr

Rose Murphy, "The Milltown Lass"
Photo: David Baker, courtesy of Topic Records

By the time Lucy was eleven and started learning fiddle she had a great store of tunes in her head. And that's what playing by heart is about: an internal model of the tune guides your fingering and bowing, just as written notation does. This mental model of the tune can develop at any time - even in your sleep! Traditional musician, singer and storyteller Packie Byrne told me:

> Sometimes, you know, I would wake in the night with a song or a tune going round in my head. 'Twould be mostly a tune I had heard for the first time and it would just click - part of it would sink in. I would have no thought of it when I went to bed, but I would wake with this tune turning round in my head and I was stuck with it! Probably it wouldn't be exactly as I heard it played but, as my father would say, the bones of it would be there.

If you *are* learning tunes from a book - as I hope you will be from this one! - try to memorise them. Listening to the Learning Discs should help. Much of the character of traditional music - and much of the pleasure - comes from the freedom with which it's played. Irish fiddle music has three variable elements - bowing, ornamentation and melody - and, by juggling them, the experienced player can generate countless variations within the parameters of the style. The starting point for improvisation of that kind is a strong sense of the tune *inside* you.

Of the published collections of Irish tunes, Breandan Breathnach's three-volume *Ceol Rince na h'Eireann* (Dance Music of Ireland) is highly regarded, though it is to the work of Francis O'Neill, mentioned earlier, that older players are usually referring if they talk about 'The Book'. Not that even *O'Neill's* is much used as a primary source. Traditional players use tune-books mainly just to jog their memory, for as O'Neill himself put it: "Memory is capricious and preserves a baffling independence of the will."

The structure of Irish tunes

Several factors make learning tunes easier than you might think. The first is understanding their structure. Most tunes have two sections, an A-part and a B-part, each consisting of eight bars of music. Each is played twice. So the structure of the tune is AABB. If it has three parts it will be played AABBCC. There are exceptions but that is the general rule.

Each section of the tune consists of four two-bar phrases. These are like question and answer. For example, here is the A-part of *Old Joe's* jig:

14

Even at a glance it is clear that there's a lot of repetition! The first and third phrases - the 'questions' - are almost identical. The second and fourth phrases - the 'answers' - are also similar, though the fourth phrase has a modified ending.   The B-part of *Old Joe's* is just as easy. In fact you have only a handful of short phrases to learn and string together and there's your tune! Not all are as simple as *Old Joe's,* though a great many are. But the principle of learning two-bar phrases - or maybe four-bar phrases once you are more used to the idiom of the music - will take you a long way.

Dance music - Accents and weak notes

Learning tunes also becomes easier if you understand the nature of dance music. With the obvious exception of slow airs, Irish tunes are always played *as if* for dancing, whether in fact there are dancers present or not. And in dance music, where a strong, infectious rhythm is the priority, the notes are not all of equal importance. Some are strongly accented while others are almost thrown away. In a double jig, for example, only the first of each group of three quavers (eighth notes) is stressed. Here's a 'skeleton' version of the A-part of *Old Joe's*:

Note the bowing. The accented notes occur on Down-bows and Up-bows alternately - and will continue to do so even when the missing 'weak' notes are put back. (Some slurs are also used to keep this alternation of Downs and Ups). The dance fiddler's bowing is never random but actively brings out the rhythm of the tune. The accents may coincide exactly with the basic pulse - as here - or they may be distributed in a more varied way, for example, falling on the off-beat.

Irish music makes no use of dynamics - the louds and softs, crescendoes and diminuendoes - of classical violin; the whole tune is played at the same 'level'. But within every phrase, every bar of music, there is this marked contrast between strong (loud) and weak notes. Attention to the fingering of the 'skeleton' notes helps both in memorising a tune and in playing it up to speed. Have you ever crossed a river on stepping stones? If you looked at every wave and pebble you'd soon lose your footing; keep to the stepping stones and it's easy to move briskly forward.

Tone and resonant notes

The tone, the quality of sound, produced by the traditional fiddler is not the same as the violinist's. An important difference is that *vibrato,* the rapid sharpening and flattening of a note by means of a subtle 'wobble' of the finger or hand, is not traditionally used in Irish playing, not even for airs. It's an odd thing but, while violin music relies on vibrato for much of its sweetness, warmth and expression, in traditional playing it sounds merely vulgar. (Conversely, the use of a *slide* - starting a note flat, then sliding it up to pitch - is part of the accepted idiom of Irish music but sounds out of place in classical violin.)

The absence of vibrato does not mean, however, that the fiddler's tone is dull, because vitality of tone can also be produced by exploiting the fiddle's natural resonance. Play the note D, for example, on the A-string with a short, strong bow-stroke, letting the bow stop on the string. Provided your third finger is accurately placed you will hear a kind of echo of the note, a sympathetic ringing of the D-string. If your third finger is even a fraction sharp or flat the tone will be dead, with no further sound once the bow has stopped. (This is also a useful objective test of how accurate your intonation is.)

There are several such *resonant notes* on the fiddle - in fact, any G, D, A or E, whether below or above the relevant open string, can set off a ringing vibration. Traditional players, used to relying on their ear for guidance, tend to play accurately in tune and their use of these resonant notes is probably what gives the live, clear sound of good fiddling. Many traditional fiddlers tend to bow somewhat nearer the fingerboard than to the bridge and this produces a soft, almost husky tone. Also, compared to violinists, they tighten up the bow less, particularly for the playing of airs.

Traditional hold

It is sometimes maintained - often most dogmatically by those who don't play the instrument! - that there is only one 'traditional' method of holding the fiddle and bow. In my view the quality of the sound and the comfort of the player are what's important. It's true that, compared with violinists required to play in the higher positions, fiddlers usually hold the violin further to the front of the body and less out to the left, perhaps also with more of a slope down towards the scroll. That seems natural enough to me and I do the same. Some older players also collapse the left wrist, taking the weight of the fiddle on the heel of the hand. 'Traditional' or not, I find this restricts the mobility of the fingers, particularly the fourth, and prefer to keep my wrist relaxed but straight. I also use a shoulder rest but there are many players who do not.

As for the bow hold, the bow in Irish fiddle playing always stays on the strings - no *spiccato* or other off-the-string techniques being used - so a greater variety of holds will work than in other types of playing. I've heard good music from players who hold the stick between just the thumb and index finger; and others who hold it like the end of a shovel! But again, personally, I prefer a standard hold.

Most traditional players use steel strings (that is, steel wound around a steel core, rather than around a gut or synthetic gut core) with fine tuners on the tailpiece. Standard tuning (A = 440) is used.

It's all in the bowing

When I was first learning Irish tunes a traditional fiddler, Sean McLaughlin, invited me to his house for whiskey, hot water and fiddle music. His own playing was full of lift and enjoyment, while mine sounded very stilted. "It's all in the bowing, Pete," was Sean's laconic explanation. And so it is. The alternation of weight and lightness, of strong and weak beats, is what dance fiddling is essentially about. Watch a good fiddler's bowing action and see how the arm's weight bears down on the string, then lifts again, up and down in constant play with the force of gravity. The *vertical* dimension of the bowing is as much in evidence as the *horizontal* movement across the strings, resulting in a series of circles, scoops and ellipses, a free-flowing arabesque of wrist movements.

In this book it is the study of *bowing patterns*, step by step from the simple to the more complex, that dictates the sequence in which the tunes are given. We'll work at first on relatively simple examples of each of the main types of tune - jig, reel, polka, hornpipe etc, exploring further bowing possibilities later. Do try to follow my bowings as exactly as possible. It is not that they are the only ones possible. And indeed any 'rules' are only provisional. But learning these bowing patterns will in the long run increase rather than limit your freedom as a player. To highlight its importance each new bowing pattern or technique is put in a 'bowing box'.

Hard and soft accents

Producing an accent with the bow involves the use of both arm-weight and speed. We'll explore both later, but here I want to suggest that there are two types of accent. What I call a *hard* accent can occur on either a Down-bow or an Up-bow but it's always at the <u>start</u> of the stroke. The bow bites into the string. Practice this on an open string, leaving a gap of silence between the notes:

What I call a *soft* accent can also occur on either a Down-bow or an Up-bow but it happens in the <u>middle</u> of the stroke. In other words, the stroke begins slowly and lightly; then comes a surge of speed and weight for the accented note, followed by a dying away. Try this example, making the first-finger note at least twice as loud as the others:

In Irish fiddling the use of a soft accent is often supplemented by a slide, grace-note or other left-hand ornament. But we'll look at all that in due course.

17

Scoil Samhraidh Willie Clancy 1989

SEVENTEENTH ANNUAL SUMMER SCHOOL

**Earlamh na Scoile (School Patron)
Dr. Padraig O hIrighle
President of Ireland**

1ú Iúil - 9ú Iúil
(1st July - 9th July)

Dance music - speeds

Here is a guide to the tempo at which each type of dance tune is played.

Double Jigs . . . . ♩. = 126
(for a 'slow jig' . . . . ♩. = 80)

Reels . . . . ♩ = 112/120

Hornpipes . . . . ♩ = 92
(for a 'slow hornpipe' somewhere between ♩ = 54 to ♩ = 84)

Polkas . . . . ♩ = 132/138

Slides . . . . ♩. = 132/138

Slip Jigs . . . . ♩. = 144

Mazurkas . . . . ♩. = 63

Highlands . . . . ♩ = 88

This is how fast the tunes should be played <u>eventually</u>. It takes time to learn to bring out in your playing all a tune's subtle internal rhythms and these should never be sacrificed to mere speed. Some teachers for that reason discourage their students from taking part in sessions - where the tendency is to play very fast - until they have been playing Irish music for at least a couple of years.

Still, once you have mastered the tune, playing up to speed does become an issue. I've already mentioned feeling the strong beats as a way of freeing up the forward movement of the music. But the real key is *economy of effort*. Any chronic tension in the way you hold your fiddle or bow will cause you problems. Are you pressing down on the fingerboard harder than necessary? Those who started violin as children, when it felt much harder to hold down a string, are likely, as adults, to be using excessive pressure. Again, how high do you lift your fingers <u>off</u> the string between notes? Take the time to discover the minimum required to clear the string. In a seasoned player you'll see scarcely more than a ripple of movement in the left hand. With bowing, too, faster playing requires smaller movements. In *Jigs 1* I recommend using ten inches of bow for the strong notes, half an inch for the others - but that's while you're learning. At speed, while the ratio will be the same, you will need to use maybe only a third or a quarter of that amount of bow. Less, as they say, is more.

Modes in Irish music

Anyone familiar with written violin music but not with folk music may be perplexed by some of the key signatures used. This is because Irish tunes are not constructed within the diatonic (major and minor) idiom of classical music but in the older system of modes. It is not necessary to understand the theory of modes to play the tunes and you may prefer to skip this section. But four modes are used in Irish music, two that sound 'major', two that sound 'minor'. They are called the Ionian, Mixolydian, Dorian and Aeolian modes and correspond to the scales you'd get if you played only the white notes of a piano, starting on C, G, D and A respectively.

The *Ionian* mode sounds exactly the same as the major scale and is the most common - over half the tunes here are in the Ionian mode. The *Mixolydian* mode resembles the Ionian but includes a minor seventh. *Tom Billy's* jig, for example, is in the Mixolydian mode of A and has a G natural instead of G#. Its key signature - two sharps - does not indicate the key of D major.

The Dorian and Aeolian modes are alike in having a minor third, but are distinguished by having a major sixth and a minor sixth respectively. *Cooley's Reel*, for example, is in the Dorian mode of E and has two sharps, F# and C#. *The Rights of Man* is in the Aeolian mode of E and, with a C natural instead of a C# as its sixth, has a single sharp as its key signature.

Some Irish tunes are constructed on gapped scales. They have only six rather than the usual seven different notes within an octave. The third is missing, for instance, from *The Walls of Liscarroll* while *Brian Boru's March* lacks the sixth and both have a rather archaic sound. Another very ancient feature of the scales used in some Irish music is the inclusion of 'half-sharp' notes - quarter tones mid-way between natural and sharp. These usually occur on the third or sixth of the scale. They cannot, of course, be played on keyboard instruments but they can on the fiddle and we'll take note of them in due course.

Chords are given for all the tunes in this book. In purely traditional playing chords are not used; all the instruments just play the tune in unison. And it is one of the beauties of Irish music that a solo fiddler or piper can deliver a tune that is complete in itself. It is widely accepted these days, however, that sensitive chordal accompaniment - on guitar, bouzouki, cittern or the like - can add something of value. The chords given in letter form are only suggestions and should of course be adapted according to taste.

Regional and personal playing styles

I've used phrases like 'Irish fiddle' and 'the tradition' as if there were but one way to play the music. The truth is that like all folk traditions Irish fiddling is extremely diverse, varying greatly from region to region and from one player to the next. Regional styles are less distinctive today than they were before the advent of recording and broadcasting, but I was intrigued by a comment Packie Byrne made to me:

> People will say: 'How the hell can you know a Sligo fiddle player from a Donegal fiddle player, or a Derry piper from an Antrim piper?' But you can, because that was always how you heard the Sligo musician play.
> And down to this very day - like, I remember the grandfathers playing fiddles and now their grandsons are playing - I bet I could almost tell you, well, to the small area, where they come from.

It may once have been the case that for each of Ireland's thirty-two counties there was a local fiddle style, as Sean O Riada suggested in a series of radio broadcasts in 1962. But some counties have at times achieved greater prominence than others. The fluid, highly ornate *Sligo* style exemplified by the fiddle playing of Michael Coleman, James Morrison and Paddy Killoran was massively influential in the early/ middle years of the twentieth century, as a result of the 78rpm records they made in America. That influence has continued strongly on both sides of the Atlantic, underlying, for example, the hard, jewel-like brilliance of players like Frankie Gavin.

The tradition of *Sliabh Luachra* - pronounced *Shlee-av Loo-kra* ("The Rushy Mountain") - on the Cork/Kerry border, with its repertoire of rare slides and polkas, gained wider currency in the1970s through the recordings of fiddlers

IRELAND

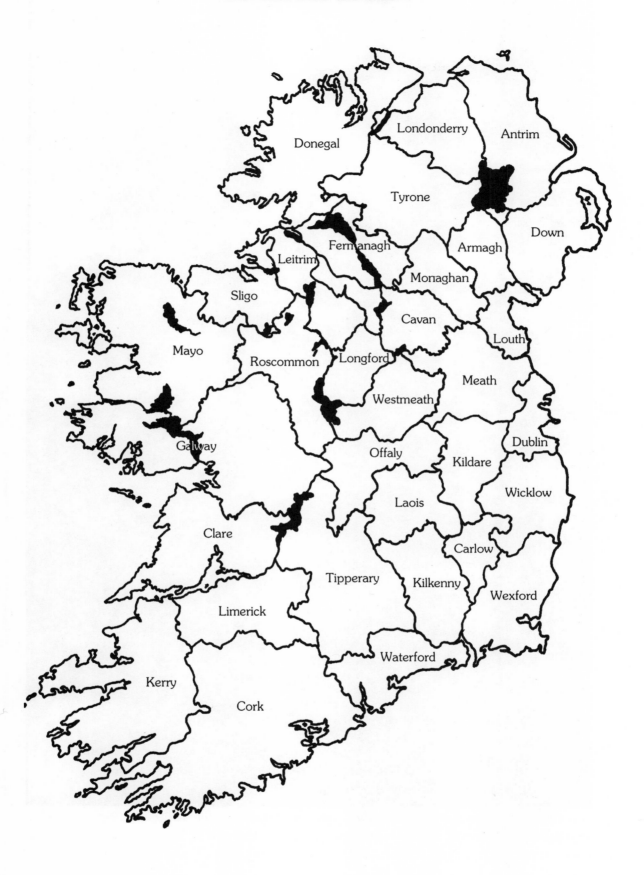

A young Kevin Burke and unidentified woman fiddler, London 1969
Photo: John Harrison

like Padraig O'Keefe, Julia Clifford and Dennis Murphy. *Galway* fiddlers including Paddy Fahy and Aggie Whyte, though not commercially recorded, have similarly made some impact beyond their immediate locality, influencing players like Kathleen Collins in America and Lucy Farr in England. Perhaps more generally pervasive has been the *West Clare* style, not unlike that of Sligo but more strongly rhythmic in character. Typified by the playing of John Kelly (and his sons, 'young' John and James), Junior Crehan and Bobby Casey, it was promoted in the 1950s by the Comhaltas Ceoltoiri Eireann.

In recent years the *Donegal* style, associated with John and Mickey Doherty as well as James Byrne, Vincent Campbell and others, has exerted a wide influence through younger players like Mairead Ni Mhoanaigh. Donegal fiddlers have a high-energy style, spacing their notes evenly, with little of the 'swing' or 'lilt' used elsewhere and using 'single-note' bowing. The Donegal tradition is strongly in the background of two of my favourite contemporary fiddle players, Paddy Glackin and Tommy Peoples. Peoples, though resident for many years in County Clare, is originally from St. Johnston, just over the border from Derry City. And in Northern Ireland, too, of course, traditional music is played - not only by Catholics, though groups like the Antrim and Down Fiddlers Association prefer to keep a low profile, since their music is widely - if mistakenly - perceived as 'nationalist'.

Beyond a certain point the artistry of good players transcends regional labels. And while it is tempting to link playing style to geographical area, differences exist between individuals, however close to each other they may live. Musical style is not a spontaneous, natural outgrowth of the soil but, at least partly, the product of conscious artistic decision. Thus it's hard to relate the playing of present-day fiddlers like Kevin Burke, for example, to any particular local style. And the broad church of Irish music includes individualists as diverse as Tommy Potts and Sean MacGuire - both, in their very different fashions, out on their own. There is always a tension in traditional music between the individual and the collective, some players tending towards innovation, others being more conservative; and a healthy tradition has a place for both.

And what, finally, of the style of the tune settings given here? They are a reflection of my own playing style, of course. This in turn has been strongly influenced by the many players I have learned from and I have credited individual sources where it has seemed meaningful to do so. A tuition package like this is inevitably a compromise between the pedagogue's desire for a logical musical system and the anarchic proliferation of a real living tradition. The 'system' is intended to keep the frustrations of learning a complex skill within tolerable limits. But listening to traditional fiddlers - whether at a big concert in town or sitting in a bar in the kind of out-of-the-way place my old Irish neighbour Rose refers to as 'Bally-go-Backwards' - is the only way to fill out the picture. A course like this can only be a sort of springboard but my hope is that by the end you will feel more confident to jump off and find your own way.

- Peter Cooper, London, September 1994

JIGS 1

Then a fig for the new fashioned waltzes
Imported from Spain and from France
And a fig for the thing called the polka,
Our own Irish jig we will dance.

- Author unknown.

The jig is the oldest type of dance tune in Ireland and has been popular since the eighteenth century or earlier. The jigs we start with are called common or double jigs, the term 'double' being derived from the 'doubled battering' step used in the dance. They have two beats to the bar and each half of the bar is usually divided into three quavers (eighth notes). The first of each group of three is accented.

Basic Jig Bowing

Bowing each note separately, notice the alternation of Down-bow and Up-bow accents. Use a longer - and therefore faster - stroke for the accented note than for the two notes that follow. Really exaggerate this at first, using nine or ten inches (23 - 25 cm) for the strong note, half an inch (1 or 2 cm) each for the others.

You may find it useful to think of two distinct points on the bow - Point A near the middle of the bow, Point B nine or ten inches towards the tip. For the first accented note the bow travels from A to B. The next two quavers require no more than a tickle up and down. For the second accented note the bow travels all the way back to Point A, again followed by a quick back-and-forth tickle.

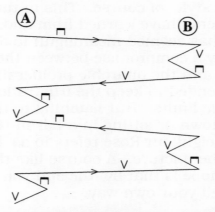

You can also let the *weight* of the arm bear down on the string to increase the accent, lightening up for the shorter strokes. Aim for the maximum contrast between strong and weak notes.

Irish tunes are usually played two or three times through, with repeats. Remember that playing in tune and with a steady rhythm is more important than playing fast.

Paddy Glackin, 1992
Photos: Rik Walton

1 THE IRISH WASHERWOMAN

If there is one tune that announces the stereotype of *Irishness* it is *The Irish Washerwoman*. Used as background music for performances of every kind, from the stage-Irish caricature of Old Mother Riley in Music Hall days to the famous 'Irish' movie *The Quiet Man* starring John Wayne, it has long been the best known of all Irish jigs. Yet, in spite of apparent over-exposure, it remains perennially popular with fiddlers and was recorded as recently as 1991 by Paddy Glackin on his album *In Full Spate* (Gael-Linn CEFCD153). The bowing here is one-stroke-to-a-note. The two quavers before the first bar-line (known as *pick-up* notes) are not accented.

Basic Jig Bowing with Slurs

In jig-playing we sometimes also use Down-bow **slurs**. These allow you to keep to the alternation of Down- and Up-bows on the main beats despite variations in rhythm. It is the <u>second</u> of the two slurred notes which is accented, so start with a short, light stroke, then increase its speed and weight. (The change from one to the other should be smooth and continuous). This is an example of what I call a *soft accent*. Here is a practice exercise:

Now try the next jig.

2   THE WALLS OF LISCARROLL

Liscarroll is a town with a ruined castle in Co. Cork. This jig has a melodic range of just over an octave and is constructed on a gapped scale that gives it an archaic sound. Note that the B-part ends differently the second time through.

The Slide

The **slide** is a common form of left-hand ornamentation and gives extra emphasis to a note. To slide a note, place the finger about half a tone flat, then slide it up to pitch. The trick is to bring the finger in at a low angle, like a plane landing on a runway. Try using a slide at the start of the next tune, *Old Joe's Jig,* pushing the first finger from around F-natural up to the F-sharp. You can also slide up to the B in bar A3.

3 OLD JOE'S JIG

A more modern-sounding tune than *The Walls Of Liscarroll*. Once you've learned it you could try playing both tunes **as a set**, ie. go straight from the first (played, of course, two or three times) to this one. A slide up to the F-sharp at the start makes the most of the change of mode into D major. At the very end of a set many fiddlers like to finish on a Down-bow, which you could do by following the bowing in the "End" bar.

"The Old Irish Jig"
- thanks to Kevin Burwood

The Grace Note

A **grace note** is another way of adding emphasis and is indicated in written music by a smaller note preceding the note being 'graced'. An example occurs in bar A4 of *My Darling Asleep.* The grace note (A) is played in the same Down-stroke as the principal note (G) and is extremely short, almost subliminal. Strictly speaking, its time is borrowed from the note before so that the principal note still falls exactly on the beat. Notice that when it is a <u>first finger note</u> that is being graced - as in bar B2 of *My Darling Asleep* - it is still the <u>third finger</u> that, in Irish music, is used for the grace-note.

4 MY DARLING ASLEEP

The last note of each section is written as a crotchet with a dot in brackets, because its length depends on which part of the tune follows. Before the B-part, which does not begin with a pick-up note, it lasts a full beat. Before the A-part, which does, it's a fraction shorter.

Melodic Variation

When a tune is repeated, a traditional fiddler will rarely play it in exactly the same way. Some variation will be introduced - by design or accident! For example, you could substitute a B for the E in bar B4:

Even changing just this one note pleasingly alters the phrase. For bar A5 or B5 you could substitute a straight descending run:

As you memorise the tune, be aware of these alternatives. A traditional fiddler not only plays the tune but plays *with* it.

Slurring together three quavers

In bars A3 and A4 of the next tune, just for variety, we slur three quavers instead of bowing them one stroke to a note. Each slur stroke - a Down-bow in the first case, an Up-bow in the second - starts on a main beat so the *hard accent* feel is no different from what we're used to. The change does not interrupt our basic alternation of Down- and Up-bow accents. Because the effect is smoother, however, a traditional fiddler might avoid sounding too bland by inserting grace-notes, as shown. Note that bow-strokes lasting one full beat each are also used in the first bar of the tune.

Link

5 GILLAN'S APPLES

If you play *Gillan's Apples* on its own, start with the high G. If you play it as a set with *My Darling Asleep*, use the 'Link' bar given above.

End

30

HORNPIPES 1

Irish dancing reached the height of its perfection in the solo
or step dances...The last quarter of the eighteenth century
seems the most likely period for their invention, and there can
be little doubt we owe their existence to the dancing masters.
The principal step dances are the jig, reel, and hornpipe.

- Breandan Breathnach, *Folk Music And Dances of Ireland*

The dancing master...would at the conclusion of the little festivity
desire them to lay down a door, on which he usually danced a few
favorite hornpipes to the music of his own fiddle.

- Francis O'Neill, *Irish Minstrels & Musicians*

Hornpipes probably originated in England but have long been part of Irish
musical tradition. Like jigs, they have two beats to the bar but each beat is
divided into **four** quavers:

The time signature for hornpipes - and, as we shall see, for reels too - is Cut
Time, which is like 4/4 time but emphasises the two-to-a-bar pulse. The
hornpipe is not played strictly as written, ie. with all the notes of equal
length, but with a distinct **bounce** or **swing.** The example given above
actually sounds like this:

That is to say, the first of each pair of quavers (eighth notes) is played *twice
as long as the second.* Thus the start of Harvest Home, although written as
straight quavers, is played:

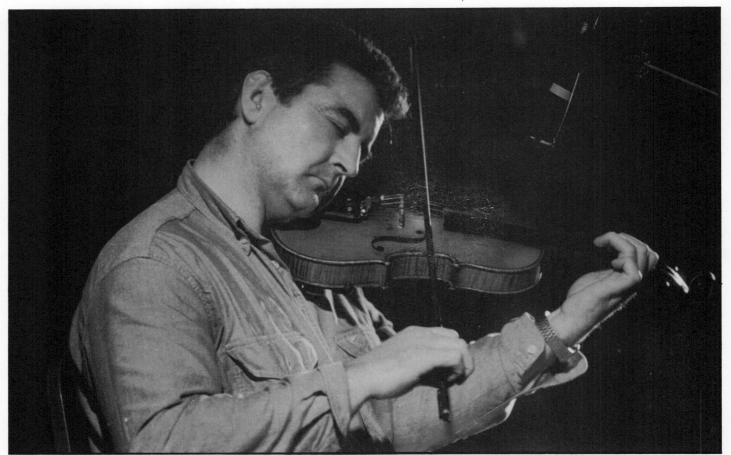

Tommy Peoples   *Photo: Seamus Murphy*

Maire O'Keefe   *Photo courtesy of Gael Linn Records*

32

In this chapter we'll look at two important bowing patterns - what I call the **One-Down Three-Up** and the **3-3-2** patterns. These are essential not only for hornpipes but for reels as well. We'll also encounter some new ornaments, the **Treble** and the **Cut**. But first, an easy technical exercise...

Wrist Circles

Bar A1 of the first hornpipe, *Harvest Home*, consists of eight notes played with simple back-and-forth bowing, one-stroke-to-a-note, starting on a Down-bow. Remember that the first note of each pair is played twice as long as the second and also that the accent falls on the first of each group of four.

As you play the phrase you will see that your bowing wrist is making a **clockwise circle**. A relaxed, flowing movement of the wrist will produce a rhythmic, musical phrase. A jerky, angular movement will make a thin, jagged sound. It is also worth noting that as you play faster the wrist circle will tend to become smaller.

Bar A3 presents a similar group of notes. Exactly the same points apply concerning rhythm and accent but the wrist circle this time is in an **anti-clockwise direction**.

Master and pupil: Sean MacGuire and Gina, Dublin 1993   Photo courtesy of Sean MacGuire

33

One-Down Three-Up Bowing

Sometimes an accented quaver played with a Down-bow is followed by three quavers slurred in an Up-bow - **One-Down Three-Up** for short. In bar A2 of *Harvest Home* this happens twice in succession:

Use a fast, heavy Down-bow for each strong beat so that you have plenty of bow left for the slower 3-note slur that follows. The Up-bow should be virtually weightless, more a reflex of the arm than a push. Note the use of a **grace note** to keep it snappy.

The Treble

The term **treble** is used to indicate a triplet whose three notes are of the <u>same pitch</u> and which are <u>bowed separately</u>. Examples occur in bars B1 and B2, where the treble is bowed Up-Down-Up. It is an important ornament, widely used by some players, notably the great Tommy Peoples, to give a stammering, staccato quality to their playing, perhaps in imitation of the sound of the uilleann pipes. It highlights or accentuates a note and can occur either on the down-beat or, as here, on the off-beat. Its effect in the latter instance is to create an **off-beat accent** which can pleasingly vary the rhythmic feel of the tune. Bring this out by really biting into the string on the first Up-bow and using short, scratchy strokes. For the pair of notes <u>preceding</u> each of the trebles we slur across on a Down-bow from the E- to the A-string.

6 HARVEST HOME

I was hitch-hiking through County Donegal in the 1970s and got a lift to the town of Dungloe. Thirsty, I went into a bar where a couple of old fellows, seeing I had a fiddle, invited me to join them for some music. I hesitated. I knew very few traditional tunes. Possibly guessing as much, one of them asked "D'you know the *Harvest Home?*" - which was a shrewd suggestion on his part. And an enjoyable (if not very long!) session of music we had before I continued my journey. It's a useful tune to know and is widely played in both Ireland and Britain.

The Cut

The cut is a special kind of grace note that separates two slurred notes <u>of the same pitch</u>, as in bar A2 of *Jackie Tar*. It feels very different from an ordinary grace note, such as that in bar A2 of *Harvest Home*. True, both ornaments occur in the same relative position in the phrase of music and in both cases a 3rd finger note decorates a 1st finger note. The bowing is also the same. What is different in the case of the **cut** is that the first finger is already in place.

Harvest Home, bar A2 - **grace note**   Jackie Tar, bar A2 - **cut**

To get a sense of how the **cut** is executed, leave the bow aside for a moment. Put your 1st finger in position and pluck the string lightly with your 3rd. Instead of placing the 3rd finger down in the normal way you will make a sideways swipe <u>across</u> the string. Now try doing this while bowing the string. That is the cut. Remember the hornpipe rhythm. The note *after* the cut is one of the longer ones so the 1st finger clings a moment before lifting off for the last note of the bow stroke. One final point: you could give an **off-beat accent** to the phrase by means of a slight increase in the speed and weight of that Up-stroke at the moment the cut occurs.

The 3-3-2 Bowing Pattern

The following bowing pattern is widely used by traditional fiddlers in both hornpipes and reels and should be thoroughly mastered. The first three notes are bowed separately (Down-Up-Down), the next three are slurred in an Up-bow and the remaining two are again bowed separately (Down-Up)*:

Note that the first accent is on a Down-bow, the second on an Up. For each of these the bow will travel, say, nine or ten inches - 20 to 25 cm, or from Point A to Point B, as we called them in *Jigs 1* - and back again. For the other notes use no more than half an inch of bow.

The second accent is on the <u>middle</u> note of the three slurred in an Up-bow. Begin the stroke softly and slowly (half an inch for the note C), then speed up for a surge of emphasis on the D (nine or ten inches) but slow down again for the last C (half an inch again): slow-FAST-slow! The final two notes of the bar of course require no more than a back-and-forth tickle.

Note that the alternation of Down- and Up-strokes on the accented notes - similar in this respect to Basic Jig Bowing - creates the possibility of strongly rhythmic playing even at a fast tempo. The alternation of hard and soft accents built into the 3-3-2 pattern also gives great vitality of tone.

Bar A7 of *Jackie Tar* offers a good example of **3-3-2** bowing.

A variation of **3-3-2** bowing occurs in bar A5 and elsewhere. Instead of slurring three quavers (eighth notes) we slur a quaver and a crotchet (quarter and eighth note) - but the *feel* of the phrase is identical.

The **3-3-2** pattern occurs also in bars A2 and A3 but <u>across</u> the bar line.

---

* It might be more logical to describe this pattern as 1-1-1-3-1-1 bowing - but too much of a mouthful!

7 JACKIE TAR

The traditional nickname for a sailor in the navy, where the dancing of hornpipes was used as a form of exercise on board ship. The tune dates from the Elizabethan period when, according to Breandan Breathnach, it was used as the air for a 'ribald' song entitled *Come ashore Jolly Tar and your trousers on.* A traditional courtship ballad known throughout the British Isles and sung to the same melody is *The Cuckoo's Nest,* by which title the fiddle tune is also sometimes known.

> 'O my darling,' says she, 'I cannot you deny,
> You've fairly won my heart by the rolling of your eye,
> It will not me surprise if your courage it should rise,
> So gently put your hand upon my cuckoo's nest.'

Double Stops

Occasionally you can embellish one note by playing another at the same time on an adjacent string. This is less common in Irish music than in some other traditions but, done sparingly, can be effective. Examples are indicated by the small notes in bars A1 and B8 of *Jackie Tar*. The small C-note in bar B5 is different - it is not played with either the E before it or the G that follows but between the two. However, it feels like a double stop as the 2nd finger is placed on the A- and E-strings simultaneously.

The commonest fault in hornpipe playing is speeding-up. So just sit on the beat, keeping it steady as an old clock's pendulum. Enjoy the easy bounce of the rhythm.

REELS 1

The Irish reel danced by Mr Coleman and Miss Gardiner
was tip-top. A member of the audience remarked that
they were very handy with their feet.

- The Sligo Times, 1912, quoted by Harry Bradshaw
in *Michael Coleman* (Viva Voce).

Probably first imported from Scotland in the 18th century, reels are now by
far the most popular type of tune in the Irish tradition, easily outnumbering
jigs, hornpipes, polkas and everything else. In sessions they are often joined
together end to end in long sets. Like hornpipes, reels have two beats to the
bar and - again as in hornpipes - each beat is divided into four:

Reels are played faster than hornpipes but are often played with the same
bouncy, swung rhythm. The degree of swing varies from player to player and
from region to region. In County Donegal, for example, reels tend to be
played 'straight' - ie with equal note-lengths. But even when they are
played with a lot of swing - with the first of each pair of quavers twice as
long as the second - their greater speed can make reels *sound* more even
than hornpipes: less bounce, more forward drive. At this stage, however,
speed really does not matter. Concentrate on good intonation, solid rhythm
- straight *or* swung - and correctly placed accents.

The reels in this chapter will require two bowing patterns we have already
encountered - **One-Down Three-Up** and **3-3-2** bowing (in various guises).
You will also recognise some left-hand ornaments we have used already -
slides, **grace-notes** and **cuts** - as well as **trebles**. The chief technical
challenge here will be an important ornament called the **roll.** But first,
some bowing technique.

Accenting a note using arm weight.

The contrast between accented and weak notes is crucial in dance fiddling. The skill of bringing it out clearly is essential if you are to play up to speed without the tune becoming horribly scrambled! There are two ways to produce an accent with the bow - with a faster stroke or a heavier stroke. In practice the two are usually combined but let's focus here on the use of **weight.**

We'll start with a <u>Down-bow</u>. Place the bow on the A-string and - don't move yet - feel the weight of your arm, hanging from the point where the bow-hair sticks to the string. When you are ready - and starting the movement from the elbow - release the weight of your arm downwards. As it drops, the bow sinks into the string, making the accent. Practice the following pattern, using the 2-beat rest to concentrate on feeling your arm weight in preparation for the accented note. Make the other three notes as light as possible:

Now, the <u>Up-bow</u> accent, which is equally important. (i) First, play a series of Up-strokes on the open A-string, lifting the bow off the string between each note and making a continuous clockwise circle. The circles made by the bow and the wrist are of course linked. Now bring the elbow too into this circular movement, so that it <u>comes in towards the body</u> on the Up-stroke, bringing the weight of the arm to bear on the string.

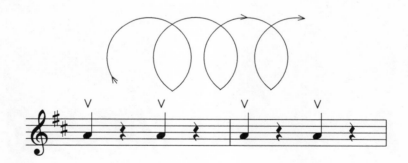

(ii) Stage 2 of this exercise is again to bring the weight of the arm in towards the body to create the Up-bow accent, <u>but without actually lifting the bow from the string</u>. Play the following, using the 2-beat rest to prepare the elbow movement. The unaccented notes should be almost weightless:

8 THE MERRY BLACKSMITH

A blacksmith courted me nine months and better,
He fairly won my heart, wrote me a letter.
With his hammer in his hand he looked so clever
And if I was with my love I'd live for ever.

                                        - Traditional song.

I was once teaching this tune to a class in which a plain-speaking woman from Yorkshire remarked: "All the blacksmiths I've ever known were right *gloomy* buggers!"

You may have noticed a similarity between bars A1 and A5 of *The Merry Blacksmith*, the dotted crotchet in A1 being replaced in A5 by three quavers. Melodic substitutions of this kind are common in Irish fiddling and bars A1 and A5 of the next tune, *The Banshee*, display a similar variation. The A-part of *The Banshee* in fact presents no new technical challenges; the bowing is **3-3-2** throughout and we use a **cut** in bars A4 and A8.

The B-part, though, does involve something new.

*Slide up to the F♯.

The First Finger Roll (∞)

The **Roll** is perhaps the most important decoration in Irish fiddling. The symbol used to indicate it (∞) is the same as that for the *turn* in classical music, but it sounds very different. The turn is graceful and melodic, the roll rhythmic, almost percussive. Here we'll learn the type of roll whose principal note - the note being decorated - is played with the first finger, in this case a B on the A-string.

The roll consists of five notes. Notice that, just as in the grace note and cut, the upper note is played with the third finger. All five notes are bowed in one stroke. For practice, try using both Down- and Up-bows alternately:

The roll lasts as long as a dotted crotchet. The exact timing of the notes <u>within</u> the roll varies slightly from player to player. As a general guide, make the first note of the five longer and shorten the next three, crowding them together, before ending with the principal note once more. It will probably help to listen to the Learning Discs.

Each of the rolls in *The Banshee* occurs on the last note of a two-bar phrase, eg B1 and B2 . The quaver D at the very end of B2 belongs, musically, to the next phrase:

So here the roll is just a flourish that marks the end of a phrase. Play the five-note sequence fluently. Keep your left thumb soft as a way of making sure your finger pressure is kept to a minimum. You can also let the bow pressure decrease at the end, so that the sound trails away:

We shall see later how rolls can be made more snappy and percussive by the use of an off-beat accent - see page 46 - but for the moment all that matters is to play the notes cleanly, without upsetting the basic beat.

There are no fewer than six examples of **One-Down, Three-Up** bowing in the B-part of *The Banshee*, each of them also involving the use of a **cut**. Can you identify them all? The first half of bar B3, though slightly disguised, is one instance. Use a swift, heavy Down-stroke, then allow the Up-bow to return almost weightlessly, as a reflex of the arm. Because of the relative complexity of this part of the tune, it may help to practice each two-bar phrase separately, <u>then</u> to link them up. Also, the A-part of this tune is easier than the B-part but, since a constant tempo is required throughout, set the overall tempo by the speed at which you can play the B-part.

9 THE BANSHEE

The banshee (from the Irish *bhean*= woman + *sidhe* = fairy) is a wailing spirit, often in the form of an old woman, whose appearance is an omen of death in the family. Her music is called, in Irish, *ceolsidhe*.

'Miss Baily and Miss Susan saw no ghosts, but they heard the summons of Ainë the banshee, before the death of their sister Kitty. This was no blood-curdling scream or trampling of horses' hoofs, but sweet sad music as of a choir singing with stringed instruments...Both sisters heard it at the same time and at first ran distractedly about to find the singing band. When they realised it was *ceolsidhe* they heard they went back to Kity's bedside and watched her as she died. Then the fairy music ceased.'

'...Ainë, the Woman of Wailing, lover of poets and learned men, the Banshee who comforts their last hours with *Ceolsidhe*, the playing of harps, wood wind and muffled drums.'

- Mary Carbery, *The Farm By Lough Gur*

Irish tunes frequently have more names than one and *The Banshee* is also known as *McMahon's* - possibly after turn-of-the-century fiddler, Professor William McMahon, 'the sweetest Irish violin player that ever came...to the Pacific coast,' according to Capt. Francis O'Neill. Or then again it may be after Tony McMahon, the present-day button accordeon virtuoso from County Clare, in the tradition of Joe Cooley. The (often vain) quest for the identity of someone whose name appears in a tune title reminds me of the old Irish couple in Brendan Behan's story, *The Scarperer*. They arrive in Paris and see the name plate on the Avenue MacMahon. '"There was them MacMahons used to live beside us in Ballybough," said she, "I wonder has it anything to do with them? One of them worked on the Glasgow boat, but I never heard of his going foreign..." The old man grunted...He didn't seem to think much of the MacMahons.'

One important point I'd like to repeat here is that reels are played with just <u>two</u>, not four beats to the bar. Thinking in terms of four crotchets is an easy trap to fall into, especially when you are learning a tune and playing it slowly. But it will seriously impede the flow of the music when we come to take it a bit faster. So in the last tune in this section consciously stress only the first quaver in a group of four:

not

10 THE MAID BEHIND THE BAR

I sometimes get my students to try singing a tune to help learn it by ear. In the case of this reel, the words of the title fit the last phrase of music so well that I wondered if there might not be an entire song waiting to be made up. One of my students, Barbara Lester, put this idea to the test and by the next class had come up with the following verses, to be sung to the A-part and B-part respectively:

> Oh there was a maid behind the bar and that was where she stayed
> Though her friends all cried 'Come out! Come out!', they never *never* could persuade
> The maid behind the bar to move - she never would come out,
> Her sole purpose on this earthly plane was serving mugs of stout.
>
> Oh unambitious serving maid, she's overworked and underpaid
> Has she no longing to be free? no existential agony?
> While serving beers and stouts to ungrateful drunken louts,
> Oh is it too late to change her fate, the maid behind the bar?

This reel, by the way, makes an excellent set with *Cooley's* (No.26), as played on the Learning Disc.

44

Jimmy Power and Paul Gross, London 1975

Photo: Tony Engle

Michael Gorman, composer of the reel "The Mountain Road," 1965

Photo: Brian Shuel

45

POLKAS

Arnoux had known several famous actresses; the young men
leaned forward to listen to him. But his words were drowned out by
the din of the music; and as soon as a quadrille or a polka was over,
everybody rushed for a table, called the waiter and laughed;
bottles of beer and sparkling lemonade exploded among the shrubberies...

Parisian dance hall, 1840s, in Flaubert's *Sentimental Education*

They were doing all kinds of nonsensical polkas
All round the room in a whirligig

- Lanigan's Ball, traditional song

The polka is a couple dance that, probably originating in Poland, spread
during the 1830s from Bohemia and through Hungary to western Europe.
By the early 1840s it was being performed at Her Majesty's Opera in London
and was the height of ballroom fashion in Paris, where polka steps became
incorporated into the *quadrille*. This 18th century dance, performed by four
couples in a square formation, had already been introduced into England
and Ireland by the soldiers of the Duke of Wellington at the end of the
Napoleonic wars. It evolved into the *set of quadrilles*, consisting of several
figures, each danced to a different rhythm - polka, mazurka, waltz etc. The
dancing of *sets*, as they were known in Ireland - or *half-sets* when only two
couples were involved - gradually filtered out from the Landlords' Society
Dances of the gentry to the houses of ordinary people. Jigs, reels and
hornpipes had come to be used in Ireland for some of the figures, but the
polka too now firmly established itself in Irish musical tradition.

The polka has two crotchet beats to the bar.   Each beat is commonly split
into two quavers with the accent on the the <u>second</u> of each pair. In other
words, it is the *off-beat* that is consistently stressed:

Unlike the quavers in hornpipes and reels, those in polkas are always played
'straight' - ie they are of strictly equal length, with no swing - unless
otherwise indicated. Fiddle players tend to slur the quavers in pairs,
starting each stroke softly, then adding weight and speed to the bow to
emphasise the second note. Practice this on the open A-string:

Down-*PULL*, Up-*PUSH*, Down-*PULL*, Up-*PUSH*

With this off-beat polka accent, the opening bars of our first polka will sound something like this:

11 O THE BRITCHES FULL OF STITCHES

This charming (and easy) tune involves only the first and second fingers of the left hand but is very satisfying to play. Note that the title fits the rhythm of the opening bars.

String Crossing

Some accurate string-crossing involving slurs is needed in both the last tune and the next one. If that feels awkward it might be worth trying this simple exercise:

In crossing from the A- to the E-string you can drop your wrist and elbow slightly; in crossing back, you raise them. Once you've got the hang of this, reverse the direction of the bowing - ie. start with an Up-bow instead of with a Down.

The opening bars of the next tune, with off-beat accent, will sound like this:

12 BILL SULLIVAN'S POLKA

With its quirky repetition of the A in the first part, this is an intriguing tune. The bowing follows a consistent pattern but if you find the slurred crossing from the E to the C# and back to the E in bars A6/7 too tricky try the alternative bowing below.

Since the 1980s there has been an upsurge of enthusiasm for the dancing of sets - and hence for the polka - throughout Ireland. For many years, however, it survived only precariously. The Gaelic League of the 1890s, having seen the ballroom sets gain popularity at the expense of the somewhat older and supposedly more 'traditional' dances likes the Four Hand Reel and the Eight Hand Jig, tried to ban all 'foreign' dances. The quotation from *Lanigan's Ball* at the head of this chapter goes on to say:

> They were doing all kinds of nonsensical polkas
> All round the room in a whirligig
> But Julia and I soon banished their nonsense
> And tipped them a twist of a real Irish jig.

Although the quadrilles had in fact been well assimilated into Irish musical tradition and were a vehicle for many old tunes, including 'real Irish jigs', as well as the newer polkas, they were replaced by so-called *ceilidh* (pronounced *kay-lee*) dances like *The Walls of Limerick, The Siege of Ennis* and *The Bridge of Athlone*. The Victorian set dances, although they lacked nationalist appeal and went out of fashion, did survive in particular localities, notably in Sliabh Luachra on the Cork/Kerry border, whose traditional musicians to this day have a rich repertoire of slides and polkas. Our next four tunes are all from that area.

Varying the accent

The next two polkas employ more varied bowings and more variety in the placing of accents. In bar A4 of the first *Ballydesmond Polka*, for example, the accent shifts to the down-beat. You will find that the Down-bow slur from A to G requires a very short, almost abrupt, bow stroke. Notice also that a 3rd finger cut is used to stress the second beat:

In this tune I use the accent symbol (>) to show where, in contrast to the prevailing off-beat emphasis, the down-beat can be stressed to good effect.

13 BALLYDESMOND POLKAS - No.1

Like many Irish polkas, the Ballydesmond polkas have a rather plaintive, melancholic quality and are, I suspect, of older vintage than the polka craze of the19th century. If so, they would simply have been converted to the polka rhythm to meet public demand. Ballydesmond, formerly called Kingwilliamstown, is a small - "Blink and you'll miss it," I was told - village in Sliabh Luachra.   These polkas are the last two of a set of three played on *The Star Above The Garter* (Claddagh, 1969) by Denis Murphy and Julia Clifford - see note on *Julia Clifford's*.

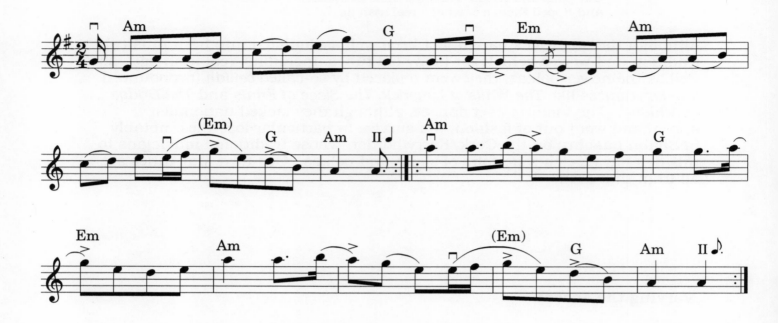

Semiquaver Triplets

A plainer version of bars A5 and B5 of the second *Ballydesmond* tune would be:

In the version given here, however, the third quaver is replaced by a semi-quaver triplet - a rounded, rolling ornament:

Cross-Bowing

Cross-bowing, a term borrowed from Scottish fiddling, consists of a succession of slurs <u>across</u> the beat. An example occurs at the end of each part of the second *Ballydesmond Polka:*

We'll also use it in the B-part of *Din Tarrant's Polka.* In both cases, it is the notes at the <u>end</u> of the slurs - ie the down-beats - that are accented.

14 BALLYDESMOND POLKAS - No. 2

The sequence of descending notes, C-B-A-G, at the start may be embellished as shown below but it's also very distinctive just as it is - especially with a Down-*PULL*, Up-*PUSH* off-beat emphasis.

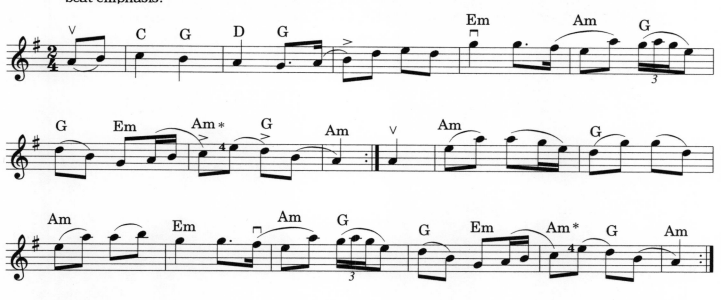

Bars **A1/2** (Embellished Version)

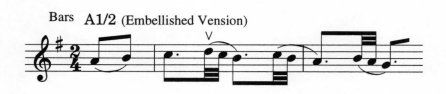

*or F

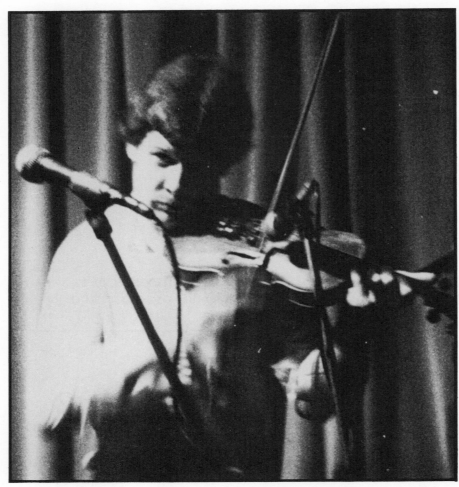

*Maurice Lennon of the famous
Leitrim family, fiddle player with
Stockton's Wing, 1982
Photo: Chris Sadler*

Sunday lunchtime session in a Camden Town pub, London 1963—Julia Clifford on fiddle Photo: Brian Shuel

15 JULIA CLIFFORD'S POLKA

Julia Clifford and her brother Denis Murphy, born in Lisheen, were, during the late 1920's and early '30s, the most distinguished pupils of Padraig O'Keefe (c.1888-1963), an outstanding local fiddle player and teacher who did as much as anyone to preserve and extend the Sliabh Luachra repertoire. Julia kept Padraig's style alive in her own playing when she moved to England in the late 30's. Later she and her husband, accordion-player John Clifford - together with their son Billy on flute - formed the *Star of Munster* trio, taking the Sliabh Luachra tunes to the heart of the London Irish scene of the '50s and '60s.

An unusual feature of this tune is the instability of the C, sometimes natural, sometimes sharp, as the tune veers between D major and the Mixolydian mode of D. Also, the repeat of the A-part is here written out in full in order to include a variant in the phrasing of the opening bar.

16 DIN TARRANT'S

Also sometimes called the *Ballyferriter Polka*. Din Tarrant, a fiddle player of the generation before Julia Clifford was, according to Alan Ward's *Music From Sliabh Luachra*, "universally regarded as a great player of polkas."

JIGS 2

Heaven reward the man who first hit upon the very original notion
of sawing the inside of a cat with the tail of a horse.

- Thomas Hood

In this section we'll look at the use of rolls in the playing of jigs - but we'll
start with a subtle change in the basic jig rhythm.

The Lilt

The quavers in a jig are not usually played exactly equally, as we played
them in Jigs 1, but *with a lilt.* In other words, the first of a group of three
quavers is lengthened a bit, the second is shortened by the same amount
and the third stays the same. Although the notes are written equal, they
<u>sound</u> more like this:

Some players, notably from County Donegal, tend to stick to the strictly
equal division of note lengths, but the lilting rhythm is more common
in most other parts of Ireland. The first of each group of three notes is
still, of course, also played with a little more weight, the other two with a
little less.

First-Finger Rolls in Jigs

The **Roll** in *Tobin's Jig,* like that in *The Banshee,* consists of five notes, the
third finger being used for the upper note, though the principal note here is
the F# on the E-string. The roll occurs twice in each section of the tune, the
first time followed by another F#, the second time by a G. Practice these on
their own before going on to the tune itself:

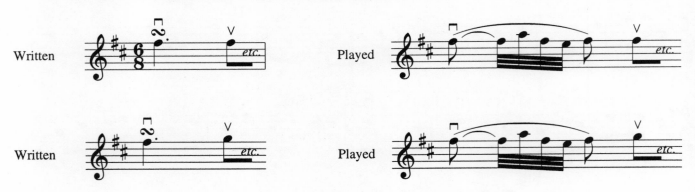

At the beginning of bar A2 accelerate the Down-bow to give the F# its proper
accent. The cut supplements it.

17 TOBIN'S JIG

One of many tunes now associated with fiddle player Michael Coleman (1891-1945), who grew up in the Killavil area of County Sligo, a locality teeming with great players. In 1914, at the age of twenty-three, he emigrated to the United States where, between 1921 and 1936, he recorded 80 or more commercially released record sides of Irish fiddle tunes. The impact of these records, both in America and back in Ireland, was enormous. *Tobin's Jig* was recorded by Coleman for the Victor label in 1927. By far the best published account of Coleman's life and career is the booklet by Harry Bradshaw, accompanying the 1991 two-cassette reissue of Coleman recordings on Viva Voce 004.

Adam Tobin, born c. 1857, played both flute and fiddle during his youth in the parish of Mooncoin, County Kilkenny, but, after emigrating to Chicago, took up the uilleann pipes. Though a late starter, he soon learned to play well. Or, as Francis O'Neill put it in his best Edwardian manner: 'Notwithstanding the disadvantages imposed by his belated beginning, he acquired very creditable proficiency in an unexpectedly short time.'

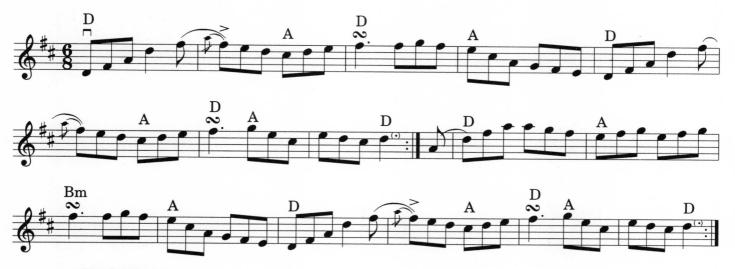

Variations

Once you feel confident with the basic version of a tune, you may feel like building in some variations. We already tried a couple of small variations for *My Darling Asleep*. We also noticed how three quavers can be substituted for a dotted crotchet in *The Merry Blacksmith* and *The Banshee*. With *Tobin's Jig* you can give the tune an interesting twist by putting three quavers in place of the dotted crotchet at the end of each section whenever you are about to repeat, or return to, the A-part:

Four Notes In The Space Of A Triplet

Another variation you might try replaces the last roll in each section. It involves squeezing **4 notes into the space of 3.** This device is frequently used by traditional musicians. Note that the last two notes of the four are slurred so that the basic pattern of accents on alternate Down- and Up-bows remains undisturbed:

MICHAEL COLEMAN
1891-1945

By
HARRY
BRADSHAW

VIVA VOCE

Michael Coleman — picture from booklet cover
Courtesy of Harry Bradshaw

2 CASSETTES   Recorded 1921-1936

JAMES
MORRISON
THE
PROFESSOR

James Morrison — picture from
cassette sleeve
Courtesy of Harry Bradshaw

Playing rolls with an 'off-beat' accent in jigs

Rolls played with an off-beat accent can give fantastic *lift* to a tune. The fingering is the same - it's the bow that imparts the accent. If you think of the rolled note as equivalent to three quavers, the accent falls on the <u>second</u> quaver. (That, at any rate, is how I play it. Other players put the accent on the third quaver - see below.) Try the bowing first on just one note, speeding up the bow to emphasise the middle note. We used a similar slow-FAST!-slow stroke in the middle of the **3-3-2** bowing pattern:

It is on this middle note that the roll occurs, so let's now add it in. Remember that, because of the **lilt** in our jig rhythm and the shortness of the middle note, the fingering of the roll is even more rapid than the notation suggests:

If you are finding this confusing, listen to the Learning Disc - your ear may be the best guide to how it should sound.

Use this off-beat emphasis for the rolls in *Morrison's Jig.* You may find it helps initially to play the opening two bars without rolls but <u>with</u> the bow speed-ups:

As mentioned above, some players prefer to stress the *third,* rather than the second quaver beat:

So the bow accent, if you play it this way, actually comes *after* the roll. It's a matter of preference.

18 MORRISON'S JIG

James Morrison (1893-1947) was another of the great Sligo fiddle players. He emigrated to the United States in 1915 and, like Michael Coleman, made fiddle recordings which had an enduring influence on the development of Irish music. Among his musical associates was a Kerry accordion player named Tom Carmody who later recalled the night before a Columbia studio recording in January 1936:

> 'Jim was up at my house...and I played him this jig. Jim asked me where I had got it from and I told him it was my father's jig called *The Stick Across The Hob*. Jim asked me to play it again and wrote it down as I played, then he got the fiddle and played it off. 'I will put that on record tomorrow,' he said, 'and we'll call it *Maurice Carmody's Favourite*'.

And so he did. Today, however, the tune is better known simply as *Morrison's*. (The story is from Harry Bradshaw's excellent sleeve notes to the reissue of the 1921-1936 recordings, *James Morrison The Professor*, on Viva Voce cassettes 001).

Note that the B- part, written out in full, is not repeated.

Where to use rolls

In a jig a roll may at times be substituted for a group of three quavers. To illustrate, let's go back to *Old Joe's* jig.

19 OLD JOE'S (with rolls)

Once you are comfortable with this new version, use the rolls more sparingly, ie. create variety by sometimes using the three notes in our original version (as I do on the Learning Disc). This kind of substitution - of ornamentation for plain note-sequence and vice versa - is the basis of the improvisatory character of traditional fiddling.

Con Curtin playing phono-fiddle (and Jimmy Power listening), London 1970   Photo: John Harrison

Michael Gorman and Margaret Barry, Keele Folk Festival 1965   Photo: Brian Shuel

HORNPIPES 2

A short, sharp-eyed hardy block of a lad came in through the doorway.
He stopped and looked around. Everyone was watching him till the dances
were over. Then he ran across to the musician, put a whisper in his ear
and took a goat's-leap back into the middle of the floor. The musician
struck up a hornpipe and the dancer beat it out faultlessly. It is wonderful
feet he had, not a note of the music did he miss, as straight as a candle,
not a stir of his body except down from his knees.

Maurice O'Sullivan, *Twenty Years A-Growing*

In this section we'll look at how to vary the basic on-the-beat accent to create more rhythmic interest. We start off, though, with a new bowing device.

Slurring Out Of A Triplet

At the end of bar A2 and the start of A3 we slur from the third note of a separately bowed triplet (F#) to the next note (G). Make the notes of the triplet very short. On the third of them, however, once you have played the F-sharp, speed the bow up, to put the accent on the G:

If this feels awkward, check that you've left enough bow for the Down-bow slur. The Up-bow slur that preceded the triplet (G to E) should have taken the bow well towards the heel and the slur <u>out</u> of the triplet merely takes us back. This is a very characteristic way of bowing triplets and trebles in both hornpipes and reels. It occurs again at the end of A4 going into A5. Contrast this with the smoothly slurred triplet that serves as a pick-up to the very first note of the tune:

The notes are identical and the accent, in both cases, is on the G that follows the triplet. At the start of the tune, however, this is a *hard* accent; in A4/5 it is a *soft* accent.

Off To California also makes extensive use of **cross bowing**, which we met in the section on polkas. It is the second note in each slur that is accented, giving the phrase a beautiful swinging rhythm. Bar A3 of *Off To California* is a good example:

Besides its steady pace and swinging rhythm, one of the main features of a hornpipe - as distinct from a reel, say - is the way it often ends with three accented crotchets. *Off To California* is an excellent example of this.

20 OFF TO CALIFORNIA

The title of this robust and cheerful hornpipe celebrates Irish emigration to the American West Coast, perhaps in particular at the time of the 1849 Gold Rush, which coincided with the Great Famine back in Ireland. It is also known as *The Humours of California* and is sometimes attributed to the Tyneside fiddler James Hill - see note on *Beeswing* (tune 56).

Rhythmic Variation

In a bar of four crotchets, an accent on the first or third note is said to be on the *down-beat*:

while an accent on the second or fourth note is said to be on the *off-beat*:

Until now we have concentrated mainly on establishing a firm down-beat accent in both hornpipes and reels, but it is also quite possible, as with jigs, to vary the accent. In the opening bar of the next tune the first A, despite being on the down-beat, is somewhat weaker than the A immediately following it on the off-beat:

When we repeat the A-part of the tune this stressing of the off-beat becomes even more apparent. Here is bar A8 followed by A1. Notice how the bowing pattern works, the strong Down-strokes corresponding to the off-beat three times in succession:

It would of course be quite feasible to change the bowing so that the accents fell on the down-beat:

but I think the first pattern makes for a more interesting rhythm.

If you wish to play *Off To California* and *Bonaparte* as a set, link them by means of a slur, thus:

21 BONAPARTE CROSSING THE RHINE

The military exploits of Napoleon Bonaparte (1769-1821) during the 1790s aroused the admiration and hopes of Irish nationalists, particularly the United Irishmen, whose leader, Theobald Wolfe Tone, pressed the French for assistance to defeat their common enemy, the British. A French expedition, with six or seven thousand troops, did indeed reach Bantry Bay in December 1796 but bad weather prevented a landing. The United Irishmen's insurrection of 1798 failed to secure widespread support in the country and was crushed.

This tune, which incidentally also serves as the air for a song about Irish road-builders entitled *The Hot Ashphalt*, employs the **One-Down-Three-Up** and **3-3-2** patterns as well as those discussed above.

* Or better, an A-chord that is neither major nor minor.

The next pair of hornpipes offer ample scope for variation.

22 THE GALWAY HORNPIPE

Recorded by Michael Coleman as *Mc Dermott's*, this is a brave, bouncy tune. Try out the variant phrases given below. The ascending arpeggio substitution for bar B4 injects an air of light-hearted swagger into the second half.

Variant A4

Variant B4

Triplet Runs

Several combinations of slurs and single bow-strokes can be used for the triplets that occur in hornpipes. In *Harvest Home* we slurred them in 3s:

In *The Galway Hornpipe* we bowed them separately, slurring out of the last one:

In *The Rights Of Man* we'll use one Up-stroke for two triplets - and the preceding quaver as well. This requires a slow, controlled bow:

There is no general rule about how triplets should be bowed. All these combinations of single strokes and slurs work well. Just be aware that the more slurs - especially longer slurs - you use, the greater the risk of runaway acceleration! It's perhaps also worth a reminder that, because of the *swing* of the hornpipe rhythm, these triplets should slip easily into the flow of the tune. For example, in *The Rights Of Man,* the quavers that follow the triplets quoted above are written 'straight' but are *played:*

In B6 there's a triplet that falls on the beat. The slur out of the triplet displaces the accent onto the off-beat note (G) that follows.

23 THE RIGHTS OF MAN

Published in two parts in1791 and 1792, *The Rights Of Man*, by the English republican writer Tom Paine (1737-1809), expressed many of the radical and democratic ideas that inspired both the French Revolution and the American War Of Independence and the young Napoleon said that he slept with a copy under his pillow. It was Tom Paine who in 1789 was handed the key of the Bastille to take to George Washington; and the French National Assembly in 1792 conferred upon him the honorary title of "French citizen." Paine's opposition to England's infamous Penal Laws made him a natural hero for the Irish Catholic majority who suffered under them.

A version of this hornpipe is played by the great Padraig O'Keefe on the Topic Records *Kerry Fiddles* album, as well as by De Danann as the opening number on their album *Ballroom*.

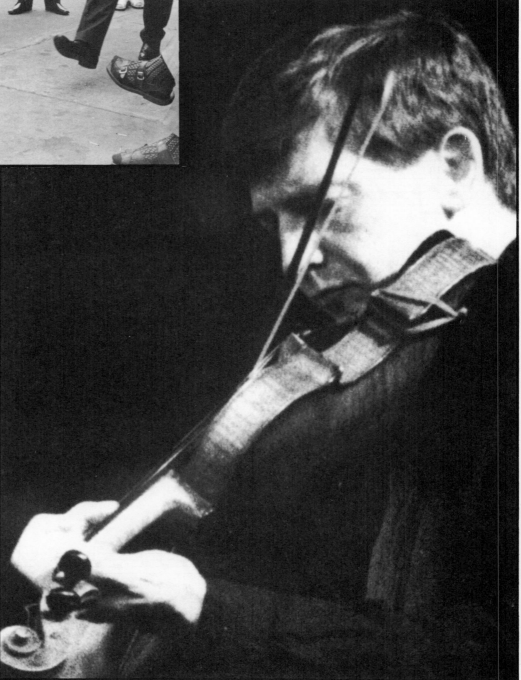

REELS 2

In the early years of the last century *(ie the early 1800s)*, the round or group dances comprised country dances and figure dances based on the solo reel and jig...The reel of three, and the reel of four or the common reel, appear to have been the first of what nowadays would be described as 'ceili' dances.

- Breandan Breathnach, *Folk Music And Dances Of Ireland*

Second and Third Finger Rolls

Like the first-finger roll, rolls whose principal note is played with the second or third finger consist of five notes: the principal note, the note above it, the principal note again, the note below it and finally the principal note once more. The notes above and below are *usually* the next notes up or down the scale. With a third finger roll, however - for example, a roll on the note D on the A-string - I sometimes catch myself using a C# rather than a C-natural for the lower note, even if the tune is in the key of G. This is not a problem since the notes of the roll are played so rapidly as to be virtually subliminal anyway. As Kevin Burke remarked in a recent fiddle workshop, you don't need to hear the upper and lower notes - the roll is essentially just "an interruption of the vibration of the string."

As with the first-finger roll, all five notes are slurred in one bow-stroke. Here is a second-finger roll written out in full:

And a third - finger roll:

More on Double Stops

There are two E-notes in bar B2 of *The Teetotaller's,* one a crotchet, the other a dotted crotchet. A bare E would be unusual in traditional playing. The first one can be embellished by keeping the first finger down from the preceding note (B) and playing on the two strings at once to make a double-stop. For the second I would use a **unison double-stop**, as indicated, sliding the fourth finger up on the A-string while also playing the open E. Until the finger has completed its slide up, there is of course a dissonance between the two, pleasingly resolved when it arrives at the same pitch.

Melodic variation again: at the beginning of bar A2 you have the choice of playing either a crotchet D *or* two quavers, D and B.

24 THE TEETOTALLER'S REEL

Also called *The Temperance Reel*. Around the turn of the 20th century, the Temperance movement, advocating total abstinence from alcoholic drink, was a major social and political force. Francis O'Neill describes a County Wicklow fiddle-player, James Whiteside, the author of songs such as "Sobriety is making way in the Ireland of today" and "Fill the bumper fair, every drop is poison". Whiteside, "dressed in an evening suit, with a tall hat, and his breast bedizened with ribbons green and yellow" would fiddle and sing his compositions to the citizens of Dublin of a Sunday afternoon, "marching up and down with a swaggering air."

In *Brendan Behan's Island* is the story of an old man from the Aran Islands, who 'was called on once to come to Dublin to some festival of Gaelic culture, to deliver a sermon or oration on temperance. He put on his best suit and he was very nervous for he had never been to Dublin before.
"How did you get through your speech on temperance?" I remember asking when he told me about it.
"Well," he said. "I brought a half a bottle of potheen with me and before I got up on the stage to speak, I went into the lavatory and had a good slug of it and it gave me the courage to go on." '

To "The Silver Spear"

70

Rolls with an Off-beat accent in reels

As we saw in *Jigs 2,* a speed-up of the bow in mid-stroke can give a snappy, 'rattling' quality to the roll. The placing of the accent, however, varies according to context. If we split the dotted crotchet on which the roll occurs into three quavers, it can be *either* the second *or* third that is accented. Not every fiddler plays rolls in exactly the same way. If in a reel we put the accent on the third, it coincides with the off-beat. Here it is in bars B3 and B4 of *The Teetotaller's Reel,* first without the actual notes of the roll:

And now with the rolls written out in full:

The accent, in other words, tends to occur *at the end* of the roll. If the accent were placed on the 'second quaver' instead - and there are fiddlers who execute the roll in that way - it would slightly anticipate the off-beat. If you find this baffling, don't worry. We are talking about very fine nuances. There are many excellent fiddlers who do not even use rolls!

More on the Treble

The A-part of *The Silver Spear* uses the treble, a device we first came across in the *Harvest Home* hornpipe. In the faster context of a reel it is hard to think of the treble as made up of three distinct, separate bow-strokes. It <u>feels</u> more as if, on the Up-strokes, you quickly tighten the biceps - or should that be triceps? - try both! - muscle in your upper bowing arm, while at the same time digging into the string. For the Down-bow slurs, of course, that arm tension is released. Have a go:

As with rolls, the effect of the treble here is to give an off-beat accent.

Double Grace Notes (Mordents)

Each four-bar phrase of the *Silver Spear* has a distinctive ending, consisting of two crotchets, B - A:

The B can be embellished with a double grace note (also called an upper mordant). It is easy to do. Having put the first finger down on the string, just make a quick, light dab with the third finger. That's it. The principal note is still played on the beat, the time occupied by the grace notes - which is only a fraction of a second - being 'borrowed' from the preceding note. (In contrast to the semiquaver triplet we came across in the *Ballydesmond Polkas*, the first note of which was the one accented.)

We use a double, rather than a single, grace note here simply because the preceding note in the phrase, D, is the same pitch as the grace note.

25 THE SILVER SPEAR

A popular tune in bar sessions. The last crotchet in bar A4 - in fact, at the end of every four-bar phrase - may be replaced by two (slurred) quavers, as indicated. Also note the variation in bowing in the B-part of the tune, with the cross-bowing of B1 being replaced by single strokes in B3.

72

Short Rolls

Every roll we've come across so far - in reels - has been on a dotted crotchet followed by a quaver:

But what if the quaver comes first, like this?

In fact, it is usually more like this:

This pattern - a quaver played with a Down bow, followed by an Up-bow roll on the next string - occurs four times in the B-part of *Cooley's Reel* and is very common. Although the crotchet, as here, is tied to a quaver of the same pitch (so that the overall duration is the same), the roll in this form is called a **short roll**. The notes are just the same as for an 'ordinary' first finger roll and the accent, the speed-up of the bow, is also still on the **off-beat**. *But the off-beat is in a different place.*

Instead of the bow-accent coming at the end of the roll, here it is the 'push' on the off-beat that, as it were, *triggers* the roll. The common temptation is to start the roll early. Just take your time and establish the quaver note on a gentle Up-bow first.

26 COOLEY'S REEL

Joe Cooley was a distinguished button accordion ("box") player from County Clare and this mighty tune is named after him. It is a favourite among traditional fiddlers. I often play it (as on the Learning Disc) after *The Maid Behind The Bar*.

Packie Byrne   Courtesy of Packie Byrne

MAZURKAS

The beat never stopped for the mazurka. Sometimes
in the highland you could ease off a little, but the mazurka
went all the time from beginning to end of the dance.
The old four-couple mazurka would be four couples
joining each other, dancing face to face. It didn't mean a damn
what you were doing in the dance, you kept the timing going...

Packie Manus Byrne, *Recollections of a Donegal Man*

The national dance of Poland is very pretty, they call it the mazurka.
It is like a galop, mixed with figures as in the quadrille, after which the
principal lady throws a kerchief in the air and whoever of the gentlemen
catches it waltzes with her twice round the room.

Mary Carbery, *The Farm By Lough Gur*

The mazurka was originally a couple dance from Poland, where *Mazur* is the
name given both to an inhabitant of the province of Mazovia and to its
characteristic dance. The mazurka spread across the whole of Poland in the
1600s and over the next two centuries caught on across Europe, becoming
fashionable in Britain in the late 1840s. Like the polka, it was incorporated
into the quadrille and many of the older Irish rural fiddle players still
remember playing mazurkas - or *mazourkas*, as the word is pronounced (and
sometimes written) in Ireland - for country house dances.

Mazurkas are in 3/4 time, that is, they have three crotchet beats to the bar.
But the rhythm is not quite that of a waltz. Some players, it is true, put
the accent on the first beat of the bar - *Um*-cha-cha - but among older
players it is often the *second* beat that is stressed.* Here is a bowing exercise
to try:

Mazurkas should be played with a relaxed, easy swing - nothing too
frenzied.

---

* Some uncertainty about the exact placing of the accent within the bar no doubt reflects
changes in the way the mazurka was danced as it migrated across Europe. Czeslaw Halski,
in *Folk Music In Poland* (Polish Cultural Foundation, London 1992), shows this process
occurring as early as 1752. The Austrian composer Joseph Riepel (1709-82) noted two
examples of the same tune, the first as it was brought by merchants from Mazovia, the
second as it was danced by the Silesians, "who by stamping feet had shifted the natural
accent of the music, and danced it beginning with an up-beat instead of the down-beat":-

(i)

(ii)

76

27 SONNY BROGAN'S MAZURKA

The late Sonny Brogan, a well-known 'box' player from Dublin, was a member of the band *Ceoltoiri Chualann* - forerunner of *The Chieftains* - in the 1960's.

28 CHARLIE LENNON'S

Dr Charlie Lennon is a respected fiddle and piano player from Leitrim, now resident in Dublin.

This mazurka is also associated with John Doherty (c.1895-1980), one of a travelling family of fiddlers, pipers and tinsmiths. Their musical legacy, dating back to the 18th century, has has had an incalculable influence on the music of Donegal. There are many good recordings of John's austere, pipes-influenced fiddling and his life and times are documented, along with those of his brothers Mickey and Simon, in Allen Feldman and Eamonn O'Doherty's excellent book, *The Northern Fiddler*.

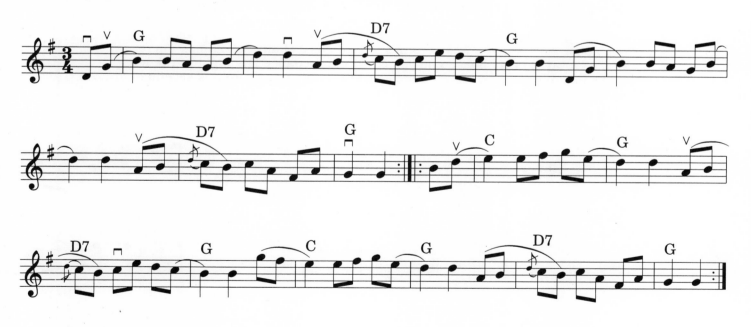

29 VINCENT CAMPBELL'S

Vincent Campbell is a fiddle player from Meenahalla, near the town of Glenties, County Donegal. He plays the previous mazurka and this one as a set on an album of fiddle music from south-west Donegal, *The Brass Fiddle*, Claddagh Records CC44. This tune is also known as *Francie Mooney's* - after the fiddle-playing father of Mairead Ni Mhoanaigh, the well-known fiddle-player and vocalist of the band *Altan*.

Joe Crane of Newcastle, England, points out that a version of the same tune is used for *Blow The Wind Southerly*, a song from the north-east of England once recorded by Kathleen Ferrier and itself originally derived from a Scots pipe tune, *Kinross of Kinross*.

30 DONEGAL MAZURKAS 1

I learned this next pair of tunes from Con McGinley, a fiddle player now in his seventies, originally from Meenacross, Co. Donegal, who described the old days:

'There was plenty of life. We used to have an awful lot of country house dancing - ordinary houses, you know. It was a great population up in our area then...and now they're all gone. Half the houses are shut up, including our house now, where I was born; it's a ruin. It's a shame, a shame...There was a crowd in every house and you could have a dance any night in the week. You could always get a crowd to dance and play music. There was seventeen fiddle players in our townland one time.'

30a Donegal Mazurkas 1 -2nd version

As previously mentioned, some ambiguity exists about the placing of the accent in mazurkas. The tune we have just learned may also played in the following way - perhaps a little closer to the Polish manner.

Con McGinley

Photo: Rob Morris

31 DONEGAL MAZURKAS 2

The Donegal fiddle style has been much influenced by Scottish fiddling. This tune makes use of a rhythmic device known as the Scottish Snap, in which a semiquaver (sixteenth note) is followed by a dotted quaver (dotted eighth note). The two notes may be bowed separately, as in bar A1 or slurred, as in B1.

The author, singing, London 1994
Photo: Warren Clarke, courtesy of In House Photography

Bobby Casey and Mike Smythe at a Camden Town pub, London 1963   *Photos: Brian Shuel*

JIGS 3

An old Tipperary man gave me a couple of tunes to learn - he had thousands of them. And being over-enthusiastic I jumped at him as he came in the door and said I'd got these three or four tunes off. But he's nudged me in the knee with his old blackthorn stick: "You're racing, sonny, you're racing," he says. "Will you slow down, for God's sake! *This* is how we play the tune." Nice, relaxed, effortless. There was enjoyment in him.

- Fiddle player Sean O'Shea, adjudicating at a London fiddle contest, 1987

In this section we'll learn our first four-part jig, but, more importantly, we'll look at a couple of new bowing patterns. The names I'm giving to these patterns, by the way, are just for convenience. Start chatting to an old fiddler about his use of 'Down-Up-Up-Down' bowing and he'll probably be very perplexed!

"Down-Up-Up-Down" Jig-Bowing

In all the jigs so far we have used *basic jig bowing,* with the two accented notes in each bar falling on Down- and Up-bows alternately. We might, for variety's sake, slur three quavers; or, after a crotchet, use a slur to restore the basic pattern. But the bowing for the accented notes has, over two bars of music, invariably followed the <u>Down-Up-Down-Up</u> sequence:

In contrast, here are the opening 4 bars of *The Lark In The Morning*, where the pattern for the accented notes is **Down-Up-Up-Down**:

True, this could have been played one-stroke-to-a-note, using simple jig bowing. But feel what a great lift the extra slurs impart. In fact, the whole first section of the tune can be bowed this way, though I prefer to revert to simple jig bowing for the last two-bar phrase. Incidentally, in the opening six bars, the slur-bows go Down where the melody goes down and Up where the melody goes up, which may make the sequence easier to memorise.

"Down-Down-Up-Up" Jig-Bowing

The next new jig-bowing pattern can be illustrated in the opening bars of the C-part of *Lark In The Morning*. It consists of putting a slur in the *middle* of each bar to link the two groups of three quavers.

Thus, if the first note in a bar is played with a Down-bow, the next accent will also be played with a Down-bow; while in the following bar, both accented notes will be played with Up-strokes: Down-Down-Up-Up. Note that the accents are *hard* and *soft* alternately. It gives a very enjoyable, rollicking feel to the music, with a lot of swing.

In introducing basic jig bowing I talked about moving from point A to point B on the bow. The new pattern involves not two but <u>three</u> such points: A, nearest the heel of the bow, B in the middle and C, nearest the tip. In the first bar, the initial note takes us from A to B; after a short up-stroke, the slur takes us from B to C, with a quick Up-Down tickle to follow. In the second bar, a fast Up-stroke - the F# - returns us from C to B; after a quick Down-bow, the slur takes us back from B to A, with a Down-Up tickle to finish. The two-bar sequence is complete.

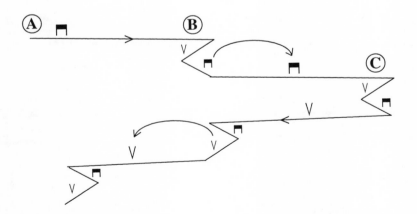

32 THE LARK IN THE MORNING

There was once a contest between two fiddlers to see which of them had the sweetest music. And there wasn't much to choose between them. They sat down in the morning and played all day, jig for jig, reel for reel, tune after tune and each was just as good as the other. Well, they continued in the evening and then had a great night of it and went right on until dawn broke. Then they both fell silent, completely played out. They had fiddled all the jigs and reels and hornpipes and everything else they knew and still it couldn't be decided which of them was the better player. In the silence they listened and they heard the morning lark above the field outside, singing away as it climbed higher and higher into the sky. And the fiddlers both agreed that it wasn't either of them that had the sweetest music - but the Lark in the Morning.

Also called *The Lark On The Strand*, this jig with its four distinctive sections, is immensely popular among traditional players.

The next three jigs also make use of the new bowing patterns, though not in so consistent a fashion as in *The Lark In The Morning*. Some of the slurs in the B-part of *The Connachtman's Rambles* are indicated with dots. It is not essential to use them - the basic pattern still works fine - but getting comfortable with the new slurs will increase your freedom of playing. Like ornaments, bowing patterns can be changed as a subtle form of variation. One such variation is built into my version of the B-part of *Paddy Clancy's*. The same note sequence occurs in bars B5 and B6 as in bars B1 and B2, but with Down-Down-Up-Up replacing Simple Jig Bowing.

33 BRYAN O'LYNN

A tune I first learned from the playing of the great Galway fiddler, Mairtin Byrnes, under the title *Hitler's Downfall*, this is in fact a very old jig which was known in the western province of Connacht as *Bata na Bplandaighe* or *The Planting Stick*. It was used for a dance in which the action of planting crops - using a pointed stick with a handle at the other end - was mimed by the dancers. Probably at a later date, it was used for a comical song, of which a couple of my favourite verses are as follows:

> Bryan O'Lynn had no breeches to wear,
> He got an old sheepskin to make him a pair,
> With the fleshy side out and the woolly side in,
> "They'll be pleasant and cool," says Bryan O'Lynn.
>
> Bryan O'Lynn had no hat to put on,
> So he got an old beaver to make him a one,
> There was none of the crown left and less of the brim,
> "Sure there's fine ventilation," says Bryan O'Lynn.

This and the next two jigs, all from the West of Ireland, have long been favourites of mine and you can hear them played as a set on my album *The Wounded Hussar*.

34 THE CONNACHTMAN'S RAMBLES

"Well, I got my pipes claned...and, to be sure, meself was in the first fashion...the lace ruffles round my wrists, that my father wore when he rattled the *Connachtman's Rambles* to the House of Commons there in College Green." Blind piper, Rory Oge, as depicted by 19th century writer Mrs. S. C. Hall.

Connacht - pronounced with an accent on the first syllable, *Conn*-ert - is one of the four ancient provinces of Ireland and it was to this poor territory that in the 17th century many Irish Catholic landowners were driven by the troops of the English general Oliver Cromwell, supposedly under the slogan "To Hell or to Connacht". To this day, the music of Connacht often seems to retain a lonesome, melancholy character. The A-part of this tune is in D, the B-part in its *relative minor*, B minor. The first note of the tune is the F# that begins the first complete bar - the preceding three quavers are played every subsequent time.

Rambling or *raking* is a term used in the Irish countryside to mean visiting with neighbours and talking, playing cards, playing music etc.

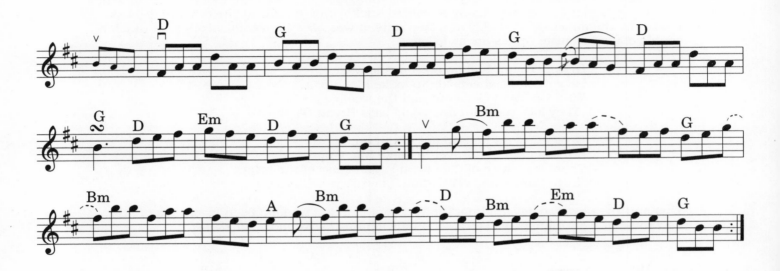

Mairtin Byrnes　　　　Photo: *John Harrison, courtesy of Topic Records*

35 PADDY CLANCY'S

Could this title refer to the Patrick Clancy of New York City mentioned by O'Neill? "Clancy's orchestra...is in much demand at balls and entertainments" and "as an Irish performer on the violin he is unequaled in that city... He fills his engagements scrupulously and to the minute - but no more. This is simply business without sentiment. Yet, when the ball is over he will visit some bartender friend and roll out jigs and reels for him until morning." The great County Clare fiddle-player Bobby Casey plays the tune on the tape *Casey In The Cowhouse*.

Variant B4

Use of 'Trebling' in Jigs

A variation of the device known as trebling, which so far we've used in a hornpipe, *The Harvest Home,* and a reel, *The Silver Spear,* can also be effective in jigs. Here's bar A1 of *The Connachtman's Rambles:*

We can play the repeated A's between the main beats like this:

It's not, strictly speaking, a treble but it *feels* the same. The F# and D are, of course, lengthened because of the lilt in the rhythm and the semiquavers (sixteenth notes) correspondingly shortened. So, as in *The Silver Spear,* make a point of digging into the string on the Up-bow, at the same time briefly tightening the muscles in the upper part of your arm, to produce the required staccato effect.

Note that both the first and second main beats of the bar are now played with a Down-bow, instead of alternating. This is not a problem here and the next bar begins, as before the change, with a Down-stroke. If, however, you ever wanted to play <u>three</u> of these trebling phrases in a row, you might need to introduce an extra slur somewhere to get back to the basic bowing pattern. Here, for instance, is the start of *Morrison's Jig,* replacing the rolls with trebles. Note the slur into bar 3.

88

HIGHLANDS

The most popular dance at the big nights when I was a kid would probably be
the highland. It was originally a Scottish dance as far as I know: in Ireland
you'd very seldom see a highland danced outside Donegal and Tyrone.
It was a pity because the highland could be a fantastic dance - a lot nicer
to watch than to do, because it was a bit strenuous to dance it. There would be
about twelve turns of the tune, it would go on and on, and in the end somebody
would drop out, and gradually there would be maybe only one or two left -
the toughest would survive!...I remember men of up to seventy, and women
the same age, they would sit down from the dance and they would be huffing and
puffing, breathing very hard, and the sweat dripping off them.

- Packie Manus Byrne, *Recollections of a Donegal Man*

Highlands, still very popular tunes in County Donegal, are related to the
Scottish strathspey and are played for energetic couple dances. Typically,
they include the Scottish Snap, the rhythmic device we came across in the
the second of the *Donegal Mazurkas*, in which a semiquaver is followed by a
dotted quaver. Highlands are played at a fair old speed and with plenty of
swing.

The bowing for the first tune is very easy - a mixture of single strokes, cross-
bowing and three-note slurs. Make the first note of the snap - eg the very
first note of the tune - extremely short.

36 UNTITLED HIGHLAND

An attractive tune that I learned from fiddler Con McGinley.

37 POLLY, PUT THE KETTLE ON

Polly, put the kettle on
O Polly, put the kettle on
Polly, put the kettle on
- We'll all have tea.

A version in Highland form of a well-known ditty that I first heard as a nursery rhyme. An American Old Time version of the same tune - entitled *Molly. Put The Kettle On* - was recorded by Gid Tanner and His Skillet Lickers.

The notes of the last bar but one are identical in each section, though for the A-part I've indicated a cross-bowing pattern and for the B-part a three-note slur. Use whichever feels more comfortable - or, if you like, incorporate the variation.

The next pair of highlands are more rhythmically varied than the last two and include some triplets.

38 CON McGINLEY'S

So called (by me) because I learned it from him. Sometimes both this and the next tune are referred to - for example, by James Byrne on his wonderful album of Donegal fiddle music, *The Road To Glenlough* - by the same title: *Jimmy Lyons'*.

If you are repeating the tune, the last note is a C. If you are ending, finish on a G. If you are going on to play the next tune, use a B, as shown in the *link* bar.

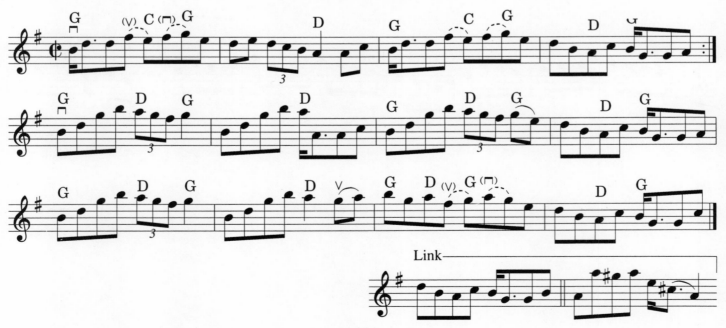

90

39 JIMMY LYONS'

The E before bar A1 is used when repeating the A-section of the tune. Ignore it when returning to the A-part from the B-part and just slur directly from the C# to the A.

The triplets in B4 are a variation that I like to use the second time through the tune.

Though in rhythm it resembles a highland, the next tune is played - or used to be played - for its own specific dance.

40 CORN RIGS

A delightful tune, little known outside Donegal. It's another one from Con McGinley.

'It was interesting to watch two men flailing corn. They stood about ten feet apart, and four sheaves of corn would be laid down between them - usually two one way and two the opposite, with the corn heads overlapping each other. One would swing his flail over his right shoulder and the other would do the same on an offbeat, which meant that the parts of the flails that was in the air, the dangerous parts, would be away from each other...It was the nicest thing for playing music to. I used to play for the threshers, keeping time with the beat; the beat of the sticks made perfect rhythm.' - Packie Manus Byrne, *Recollections of a Donegal Man.*

REELS 3

*I praise God for the gift of playing the fiddle, for I see in it
a very poor reflection of the unbroken music of Heaven.*

- Tommy Potts.

41 THE CUP OF TEA

Boyle: Pull over to the fire, Joxer, an' we'll have a cup o' tay in a minute.
Joxer: Ah, a cup o' tay's a darlin' thing, a daaarlin' thing...
    - from Sean O'Casey's Juno and The Paycock

'The tea was very important, because you drank tea all day and all night, and if you felt like
it you got up in the middle of the night and drank more tea, 'cause 'twas there! The nearest
pub to us was about seven miles, and after a hard day in the fields, to walk fourteen miles
for a bottle of Guinness or a pint of beer was a bit out of the question. So we lived on tea
instead...Some places back home, they used to make a big pitcher of tea in the morning, and
that sat on the hob all day and all night...They would take a few coals out of the fire, mush
them up and put the teapot sitting on top of the coals, and you would see the lid jumping
up and down, with the tea boiling!' Packie Manus Byrne, *Recollections of a Donegal Man.*

It's no surprise to find a tune named in honour of so popular a beverage. O'Neill quotes
what is probably an early version of the tune - a 2-part single reel called *The Unfortunate
Cup Of Tea* - from Haverty's *Three Hundred Irish Airs* while Paddy Glackin has a version
called *The Cup of (Overdrawn) Tea!*

92

Bowing an End-of-Bar Crotchet (i)

The various bowing patterns we have learned - **One Down Three Up, 3-3-2, Cross-bowing** etc - are useful in most reels, but additional slurs are sometimes dictated by the 'shape' of a particular tune. For example, several bars in *The Cup Of Tea* end with an emphatic Down-bow crotchet:

This rhythmic figure, which occurs at the end of A4, A8, B4, B8 and C6 is part of what makes the tune distinctive. The bars that follow begin with an Up-stroke (in the case of the A-part, slurring two quavers) to restore the 'normal' bowing pattern:

That is why - unusually, since there are no pick-up notes - the whole tune begins with an Up-bow slur. Note that the Up-bow slur is embellished with a double grace-note to keep it snappy.

Single Reels

Reels are described as *single* when each section of the tune has only four bars, instead of the usual eight. Or you could think of each section as having eight bars, but played without repeats - 'single'. The next two tunes are written out in full - for some variants to be built into them - so, although it will probably feel strange, just carry on to the next section without repeating.

Bowing an End-of-Bar Crotchet (ii)

As in *The Cup Of Tea* we encounter a Down-bow crochet at the end of bar B2 of *The Bank Of Ireland*. Again, we find our way back to 'normal' bowing, but this time by continuing the Down-bow across in a slur to the E-string - very satisying, provided you save plenty of bow for the roll on the F#.

42 THE BANK OF IRELAND

Originally designed around 1730 by Edward Lovett Pearce as Ireland's Parliament House, this prominent building in central Dublin - just across from Trinity College on College Green- was sold to the Bank Of Ireland in 1802, following the Act of Union by which Ireland came to be governed from Westminster. A condition of the sale was that the memory of its former functions should be obliterated by alterations. The House of Commons was duly converted into a Commercial Chamber, but the House of Lords was preserved and can still be visited.

In bars A6 and A7 a triplet and treble respectively - each of which should be played in a relatively unaccented manner - have the effect of moving the accent over onto the off-beat. We used the same device in bar B6 of *The Rights of Man* hornpipe.

The scale used in the A-part of *The Bank Of Ireland* is the Dorian mode of A, with C-natural and F#. But the latter notes - the 3rd and 6th of the scale - are unstable. The F#, in bar A4, for example, may be flattened to what is sometimes called a half-sharp - a pitch midway between sharp and natural, once widely used in traditional music and indicated here with an upward pointing arrow. (Alternatively, if you prefer, use a first finger slide.) The B-part of the tune is in D major.

Courtesy of the Bank of Ireland

Delayed Change of Note

A decorative device sometimes used by traditional players occurs in the 'variant' bar A8 of our next tune. Compare it with the 'normal' A8 and you'll see that the note G on the second main beat is held up for just the length of a quaver by a repetition of the F#. It's one of those subtle variations that surprise the ear and delight the attentive listener.

43 THE MORNING STAR

I learned this lovely reel from the playing of Denis Murphy. The Morning Star is, of course, the planet Venus. But there may also be a more local reference. In her preface to *The Farm By Lough Gur,* Mary Carbery says that 'Mrs Fogarty welcomed me to her home *(in Bruff, County Limerick)* on the bank of the lovely river Dawn, or Morning Star...'

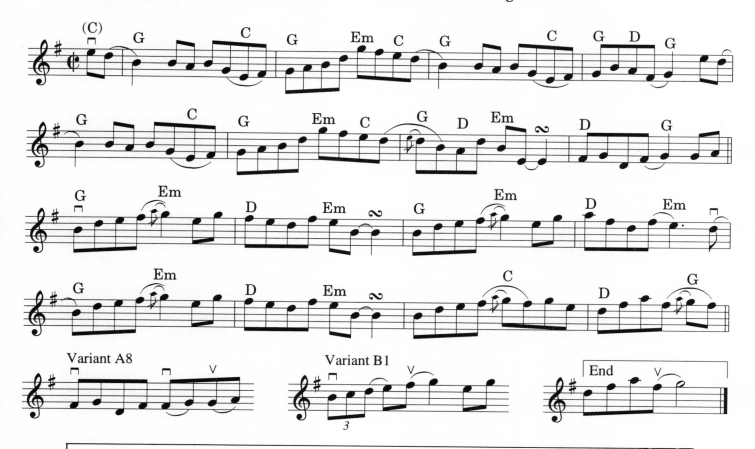

Slurs at the start or end of a section

There is often more choice as to how one bows a tune than the examples so far may have suggested. For instance, each section of the next reel, *The Musical Priest,* starts with two pick-up notes. These can either be slurred in an Up-stroke or bowed separately: Down-Up. It depends on whether you choose to bow the last two notes of the preceding phrase with or without a slur. Going from, say, the end of the A-part into the start of the B-part, either of the following bowings would work:

Use whichever one feels more comfortable.

Unless you are playing for dancers - when the number of bars being played <u>may</u> make a difference - it does not much matter whether a reel is single or double. In sessions, it is common to mix single reels in amongst ordinary 'double' reels. In the set that follows *The Musical Priest* and *The Morning Dew* are both single while *The Salamanca* is not.

44 THE MUSICAL PRIEST

O'Neill, in his *Irish Minstrels and Musicians*, lists a couple of dozen 'Reverend Musicians', among them, in the 18th century, the Rev. Charles Macklin of the Episcopal Church in Clonfert, Co. Galway whose "wit, originality and eccentricity" were expressed in "the whimsical prank of playing out his congregations with a solo on the bagpipes after the service." O'Neill notes, however, that "for this breach of religious decorum he was dismissed from his curacy."

More successful was the Right Rev. Timothy J. O'Mahony, a native of Cork, who in 1875 became bishop of Armidale, a mining district in Australia, and "laboured strenuously to gather from his scattered flock" sufficient funds to build a church. But, "although the mines were filled with Irish workmen," whenever the bishop appeared they would scatter. "At last a happy thought struck him, and the next time he called at the camp he brought with him a fiddle upon which he was an accomplished performer." He played tune after tune and "first one head appeared, then another over the knolls and hills" until, by the time the bishop reached the mine "quite a large number of the boys had gathered round. Some were crying at the sound of the once familiar airs; others were dancing with joy..." After that O'Mahony became a "most welcome visitor" to the camp and raised the money to build his church.

In the 19th and the earlier part of the 20th century the Church, as a matter of fact, far from encouraging traditional music in Ireland, tried to suppress it . O'Neill complained in his *Irish Folk Music* (1910) that the music 'could have survived even the disasters of the Famine had not the means for its preservation and perpetuation - the crossroads and farmhouse dances - been capriciously and arbitrarily suppressed. 'Twas done in my native parish of Caherea, West Carberry, in my boyhood days, by a gloomy puritanical pastor.' And years later, spurred on by the clergy, the Irish government in 1936 brought in the Public Dance Halls Act which laid down the conditions for the holding of dances. According to Breandan Breathnach, in his booklet *Dancing In Ireland*, the Act was probably not intended to apply to parties in private houses but 'the local clergy and gardai acted as if it did and by their harassment they put an end to this kind of dancing in those areas of rural Ireland where it still survived.'

By the early 1960s, when rock'n'roll established itself, the Church seems to have decided in favour of traditional music as the lesser of two evils. "Our horizons were narrowly confined," recalls Nell McCafferty of her strait-laced teenage years in Derry. "We could become nuns; failing that, teachers; failing that, it was understood though not mentioned, we might consider marriage...Of course we must have some pleasure and ceili dancing on a Saturday night met with approval. While Monica and company rocked and rolled in the Crit ballroom, I was doing the martial march of the *Walls of Limerick*, stepping it out to a tune that glorified the martyrdom of the Irish at the hands of the English in a town south of the border - the location of which I did not then know. Our wild Gaelic whirls in the parish hall were supervised by a priest." *(The 1950s and 1960s in Derry* by Nell McCafferty in *Irish Life and Traditions*, 1986).

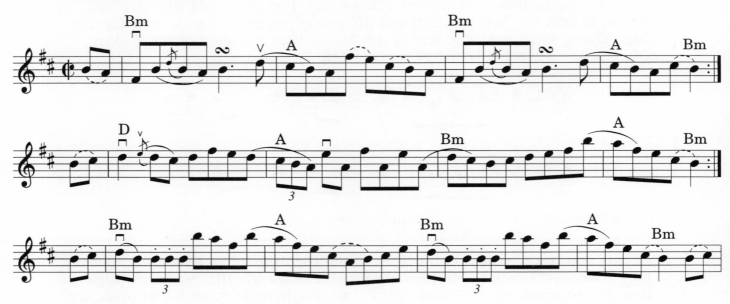

96

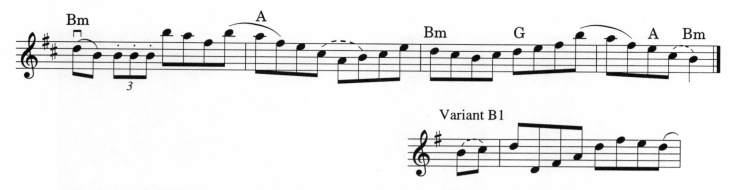

As you learn these new reels be aware of the ways in which the accent can shift from the down-beat to the off-beat. It is probably true to say that it is as much on one as the other. The skilful fiddle player varies the stress without the listener consciously noticing.

45 THE SALAMANCA

I first heard this reel on a 1975 album by *The Bothy Band*, with Tommy Peoples on fiddle. Salamanca, in Spain, has been famed as a seat of learning since the 13th century when its university was founded by Alfonso XI. Many of the Irish priest-hood were trained at its Roman Catholic seminary. In Colm Toibin's novel, *The Heather Blazing*, for example, "Father Rossiter carried down all of the old vestments from the Manse and old pictures of bishops and souvenirs he had brought home from Salamanca..." It may also be that a battle fought at Salamanca by the Duke of Wellington was the occasion of the tune's composition. PJ Curtis, in his book *Notes From The Heart*, mentions a 'spine-tingling' cylinder recording of the tune made in New York around 1898 by an uilleann piper, possibly William (Billy) Hanafin.

Wm. F. Hanafin   Michael Hanafin

Billy and Michael Hanafin   *Courtesy of Topic Records*

46 THE MORNING DEW

Also called *The Hare In The Heather* and, in Irish, *Giorria sa bhFraoch*, this is one of the great
Irish reels. Listen to as many versions of it as you can to get a sense of how traditional
musicians have varied it. Outstanding recordings have been made by Paddy Glackin - from
whom the variation for bars A5 and 6 is borowed - and James Kelly, as well as Michael
Coleman. The variation for bar B5 is Michael Coleman's - an ingenious lowering of the F#
by an octave that totally alters the feel of the phrase.

99

AIRS

Irish fiddlers are by no means few, yet
how many who revel in the airy jig and reel
can render with due expression those airs and melodies,
quaint, plaintive, and even bold,
which affect our emotions so deeply.
                    - O'Neill, *Irish Minstrels & Musicians*

The first two pieces in this section are compositions by Turlough O'Carolan, the third a traditional slow air. All are listening pieces rather than dance tunes but they differ in style. The O'Carolan tunes - even the lament, *The Wounded Hussar* - were composed for instrumental performance and have a regular pulse. The rhythm of *The Heart Is True* is very much freer, reflecting its origin in the song tradition. A traditional unaccompanied singer would vary the phrasing of the music to fit the words, whether they were in Irish or, as in this case, English. All the tunes are arranged here - non-traditionally - in three parts. For solo fiddle, just play the top line. The other parts could be played on second fiddle and cello, or on a keyboard instrument.

47 O'CAROLAN'S DRAUGHT

Turlough (or Terence) O'Carolan (1670-1738) occupies a unique place in Irish music - a professional composer and musician whose works (or many of them) have become accepted into the repertoire of traditional folk musicians. His own music grew out of the courtly Irish harp tradition, the music of a Catholic aristocracy whose power, by O'Carolan's time, had been severely reduced by the Penal Laws. But the patronage of the Big Houses, perhaps surprisingly, still allowed him to make his living as an itinerant musician, composing pieces dedicated to his various hosts. The title of this tune possibly reflects O'Carolan's reputation as a whiskey drinker. In its stately manner it has much more in common with the Italian baroque music of its day than with the dance music tradition of jigs and reels.

101

48 THE WOUNDED HUSSAR

This lament was composed by O'Carolan for one Captain O'Kane, by which title the tune is also sometimes known. O'Kane, presumably a member of a Catholic Ulster family, seems to have returned to Ireland from long miltary service in continental Europe, only to discover that, following James II's defeat by the Protestant William of Orange at the Battle of the Boyne (1690), his family's land had been expropriated. Patrick O'Leary, quoted in O'Neill's *Irish Minstrels & Musicians*, described O'Kane as 'the hero of a hundred fights from Landon to Oudenarde, who, when old and war-worn, tottered back from the Low Countries to his birthplace to die, and found himself not only a stranger, but an outlawed, disinherited, homeless wanderer in the ancient territories that his fathers ruled as Lords of Limavady. His friend and sympathizer, the illustrious Turlough O'Carolan, has immortalized his name in strains the most plaintive and touching.'

The tune has passed into folk tradition in various keys. The G minor version given here - and which I recorded as the title track of my 1993 album of Irish fiddle music - is based on that of a 19th century English fiddle player, John Moore of Shropshire, whose manuscript is reprinted in a collection called *The Ironbridge Hornpipe* (Dragonfly Music, 1991). In O'Neill's *Music Of Ireland* the tune appears in E minor. The Donegal fiddler John Doherty (c. 1895-1980) recorded a haunting version - included on the album, *Pedlar's Pack* - that seems to be played in F minor (though possibly E minor with the fiddle tuned sharp).

This is a slow piece - rather meandering, if you like - and the 6/8 time signature should not be taken to imply a jig!

49 THE HEART IS TRUE

Our ship is ready to bear away
Come, comrades, o'er the stormy sea.
Her snow-white wings they are unfurled
And soon she'll swim in a watery world.

chorus
Ah, do not forget, love, do not grieve
The heart is true and can't deceive.
My heart and hand with you I'll leave
Fare thee well, true love, remember me.

Farewell to you, my precious pearl
It's my lovely dark-haired, blue-eyed girl
And when I'm on the stormy sea
When you think of Ireland, remember me

Farewell to Dublin's hills and braes,
To Killarney's lakes and silvery seas
'Twas many the bright long summer's day
When we passed those hours of joy away.

Oh Erin dear, it grieves my heart
To think that I so soon must part
And friends 'soever dear and kind
In sorrow I must leave behind.

Peta Webb   *Courtesy of Peta Webb*

The excitement of departure for the New World expressed in the first verse gives way to the
pain of separation in this emigration ballad. I learned it from singer Peta Webb who got it
from Armagh traditional singer, Mary Toner. As mentioned earlier, a fairly free interpretation
of the time values of the notes is appropriate on an air like this, with pauses, for instance,
on significant words or at the ends of phrases. The traditional fiddler or piper would closely
follow in his or her mind the rhythm of the words while playing.

The Irish tradition is very rich in slow airs. Padraig O'Keefe and Julia Clifford, for example, both had extensive repertoires, John Doherty had some lovely ones - as indeed did most of the older players. Among present-day fiddlers listen to Matt Cranitch who, in his album of airs, *Eistigh Seal* (Gael Linn CEF 104) captures the beauty of the tunes without a trace of sentimentality. It can take a long time to develop the feeling for an air and to put it across in your playing, but it is a rewarding task.

SLIDES or SINGLE JIGS

The single jig is not unlike the double, but is modified to suit
the crotchet-quaver arrangement of the music. Thus, in grinding,
the floor is struck only four times instead of six (as in the double jig),
and in battering only twice - by the hop on the first foot and a tap
on the forward movement of the other foot. It is this single battering
which gives the tune its name.

- Breandan Breathnach, *Folk Music And Dances Of Ireland*

The men stamp rhythmically to the music at various points...but in
the ordinary way any rules there may be about the precise timing
of this 'battering' are disregarded. The set has six figures: the first
four danced to polkas (one of these is often replaced by a jig), the fifth
called the 'slide' danced to a fast single jig (these tunes are hence always
called 'slides') and the sixth to a hornpipe or reel. The whole dance is
executed at a furious pace except perhaps for the hornpipe, which
serves as a respite after the long and especially fast slide.

- Alan Ward, description of polka set in *Music From Sliabh Luachra*

The jigs we have looked at so far are *double* jigs, typically consisting of two
groups of three quavers to the bar:

The characteristic rhythmic pattern of a single jig is that of a crotchet
followed by a quaver: *

Single jigs are also called *slides* after a dance figure of that name.[†] They are
written out in 12/8 time and played somewhat faster than double jigs. It
helps the forward movement of the tune if you accent the first and third
beats of the bar:

---

*   The distinction made between a double and a single jig on the basis of its <u>rhythm</u> differs
       from the distinction between a single and double reel on the basis of its number of bars (see
       Reels 3).

†   The term *slide*, meaning single jig, should not be confused with the term *slide* used to
       denote a form of left-hand decoration (see *Jigs 1*). The terminology used to describe Irish
       traditional music is not very logical. As a friend of mine, Steafan Hannigan, remarked, if
       you'd ordered it from a shop, you'd probably send it back!

After a strong Down-stroke on the beat, taking the bow well towards the tip, you may find the Up-bow slur that follows convenient, as in the above example from *The Road To Lisdoonvarna*.

Slides are an integral part of some of the *sets* danced in Sliabh Luachra and described by Alan Ward at the head of this chapter. The crotchet beat of the polka is equal to the dotted crotchet beat of the slide, which indicates just how fast they are played!

50 TOORMORE

The tune starts, not on the two pick-up notes (A, C#) but on the E that begins the first full bar. The pick-up notes are included every subsequent time. Its title means *Big Tower* in Irish. I learned both this and the next tune from two Cork musicians, box-player Johnny O'Leary and fiddler John Coakley. You can hear it played by fiddler Matt Cranitch's band *Any Old Time* on their album *Phoenix*. Once you've learned *Toormore* try playing it an octave lower. The playing of two fiddles in octaves - 'high' and 'bass' parts together - is traditional in Kerry and in Donegal.

51 THE CULLEN SLIDE

Peggy O'Riordan's pub in the village of Cullen was by all accounts at one time a great place for the dancing of the *sets*.

The Open-string Roll

This is a useful ornament which, like the other rolls, consists of five notes:

It is played with the same time-values as the other rolls and a speed-up of the bow may again be used to impart a snappy, percussive quality to it.

52 THE STAR ABOVE THE GARTER

Played by Denis Murphy and Julia Clifford on their classic 1969 album of the same name (Claddagh Records CC5).

108

53 THE ROAD TO LISDOONVARNA

Before the Great Famine (1846-1851) it was common for an Irish farmer to sub-divide his land between several sons, each thereby having at least enough of a patch to grow a subsistence crop of potatoes. Afterwards, when this pattern had to change and efforts were made to keep the land together as a unit, it became common for the eldest son to put off marriage until he could inherit the family farm, maybe at forty or even fifty years of age. But where was he then to meet his future wife? Matchmakers had an important role in finding suitable partners and arranging the details of the match. The village of Lisdoonvarna in County Clare is still famous for its annual matchmaking ceremony, though drinking is probably the most serious business conducted there these days. Still, at one time it might have been with mixed feelings of excitement and trepidation that you'd walk down the *Road To Lisdoonvarna*.

"And," according to writer Maeve Binchy, "it's not over yet. At the end of the summer the two sexes flock into the town, with a hefty sprinkling of those already attached and not wanting to make any further arrangements. The Lisdoonvarna festival is a non-stop party, good-humoured bubbling, the ideal background to romance no matter how prosaic the elderly farmers are reputed to be in their demands and however much they are reported to prefer a potential bride to own her own tractor or combine harvester than to have golden hair and blue eyes." *(Irish Life and Traditions).*

Signpost to Lisdoonvarna
Photo: Pete Cooper

109

HORNPIPES 3

The hornpipe was usually danced by one man alone.
It was rarely danced by a woman, as the steps were regarded
as requiring the vigour and sound which only a man could
bring to them. It appears the ladies of Cork were exceptional
in that they not alone danced the hornpipe, but used the
heavier steps in jigs and reels which elsewhere were used
exclusively by men.

- Breandan Breathnach, *Folk Music And Dances Of Ireland*

All three of the tunes in this section draw liberally on the various types of
bowing and ornamentation we have already developed. The third tune,
Beeswing, is in the key of Bb - a key that is not very common in Irish
music. Apart from that, no new techniques are involved. But these are
great tunes to play, not least for the way that one bowing pattern leads into
another and - in the case of *McGlinchey's* - for its prolific left-hand
ornamentation.

Arpeggios

Much of the melody in these tunes, and in hornpipes generally, is based on
arpeggio patterns - in other words, on the notes that, if played at the same
time, would make up a chord. An arpeggio consists of the *first, third* and *fifth*
notes of the relevant scale. Here are some 2-octave arpeggios that, if you
are not already familiar with them, it would be useful to practice. For the
keys of A, G and Bb the key-note (the *first*) is at the bottom and top of the
arpeggio. For the keys of D, C, F and Eb, in order to play a 2-octave pattern
within first position, we start with the *third* or the *fifth*.

Key of A

Key of D

Sean MacGuire at home in his garden
Photos: Brendan Donnelly

Key of G

Key of C

Key of F

Key of B♭

Key of E♭

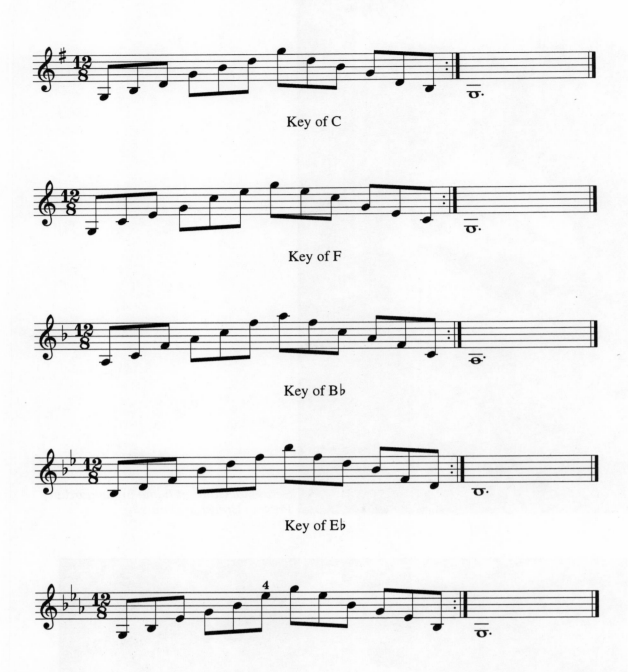

There are many arpeggio patterns in the tunes here, though the exact sequence of notes may vary. The opening bar of *The Tailor's Twist* is a good example of an arpeggio of D. I'll point out some others in the tunes that follow.

54 THE TAILOR'S TWIST

This delightful hornpipe uses a lot of cross-bowing that goes well with its lolloping, easy rhythm. Notice how the triplets in A4 and B4 create consecutive accents on the second and third beat. An influential Columbia recording of the tune - paired with *The Flowers Of Spring* - was made by James Morrison in 1935. The title presumably refers to the thread used for sewing clothes.

In former times in the Irish countryside a 'journeyman tailor' would be summoned when clothes were needed. 'The tailor would come and he would take the door off the hinges and put straw under it and sit down on it and cut and sew the garments he was to make on it. He would be several days at the job, and he would go on to another house when he had made all the clothes for you. He would be a journeyman tailor. He would hear all the talk wherever he was, and that was how tailors came to have a name for being wise men, as they are.' - Eric Cross, *The Tailor And Ansty.*

As on the learning tape, *McGlinchey's Hornpipe* follows on very satisfyingly from *The Tailor's Twist.* It is in three sections. At the start of the B-part a D arpeggio pattern (B1) is followed by a G arpeggio pattern (B2). Such patterns can be a source of variation, either by design or accident, since the arpeggios provides a secure underlying structure from which to depart from the basic melody. In the B2 variation given here, for instance, the tune descends only as far as the D instead of to the low B, so that we hit the top note of the arpeggio (G on the E-string) a fraction early. An F# is inserted to fill the gap.

Watch out for the *accidentals* - the occasional sharps and flats - in this tune.

55 McGLINCHEY'S

Also called *Cross The Fence* according to Matt Cranitch, this hornpipe was composed for a competition in 1961 by the great fiddler Brendan McGlinchey, originally from Armagh City. After an absence from the music scene of several years, Brendan recently made a welcome return, teaching, for example, at the 1993 Willie Clancy Summer School in County Clare. This is one of my all-time favourite tunes and I play it as the closing track on my album, *The Wounded Hussar*.

Brendan McGlinchey
Courtesy of Brendan McGlinchey

114

The next tune, *Beeswing*, is put together almost entirely from sections of different arpeggios, cunningly welded together like steel girders in a grand Victorian engineering project. In bars 5 and 6 of both sections of the tune, for example, is a Bb-F-Eb-Bb sequence based on alternating intervals of a fifth and a sixth which, once you've got the hang of the fingering, is particularly pleasing.

56 BEESWING

A tune in Bb by James Hill, fiddle player and composer whose other famous tunes include *The High Level Bridge* and *The Hawk*. Hill, the "Paganini of hornpipe players," was a professional public house fiddler in the middle years of the 19th century, active within the large Irish community on Tyneside in the north-east of England. This is one of several of Hill's tunes that have taken root in Irish tradition and the elaborate variation is from Belfast fiddler Sean MacGuire. Both versions - and dozens of other famous James Hill tunes - are to be found in Graham Dixon's excellent collection *The Lads Like Beer* (Random Publications, 1987).

Beeswing was a famous North of England racehorse of the 1830's and 1840's and a public house was named after it. Whether Hill named his tune after the horse or the pub is not known.

Session at The Favourite, north London — fiddler: Jimmy Power
Photo: Robert Sale

56A BEESWING

Sean MacGuire's variation (from a transcription by A.S. Robertson).

Fiddler Lucy Farr with Frances Geraghty and Johnny Gorman, London 1975   Photo: Tony Engle

Sean Keane, fiddle player with The Chieftains   *Courtesy of Claddagh Records*

SLIP JIGS

What music could be more gay and spirited than the hop or slip jig
in nine-eight time...?

        - O'Neill, *Irish Music & Musicians*

Hop Jigs, although danced as bouts *(ie solo dances)*, are mainly social dances.
They are of a simple, sprightly and graceful character and include steps and
figures; for example, the slip and side-steps for changing places...Regarding our
national dances in general, it may be observed that the Slip or Hop Jig is the
oldest as well as the most characteristic of them.

        - Frank Roche (1866-1961) *Note On Irish Dancing*
in The Roche Collection of Traditional Irish Music (Ossian Publications)

Sometimes referred to by older players as *hop jigs,* slip jigs have not two but
three beats to the bar. The greater rhythmic variation this entails makes it
hard to establish a completely systematic pattern of bowing throughout.
Although I have written out *The Kid On The Mountain,* for example, with a
Down-bow at the start of each section, I do find that when I'm playing by
heart my bowing is more random than that! You may well find that, once
you've memorised the tune, your bowing differs from what's written. This
won't be a problem provided you have developed a <u>feel</u> for jig-bowing. What
matters, as always, is to generate the correct rhythm - based, in this case,
on three beats to a bar.

"End-Bowing" in mid-tune

At the end of some of the first jigs we learned, *Old Joe's* and *Gillan's Apples,*
I suggested a bowing that allowed us to play the final note on a Down-bow.
The last two quavers in the preceding group of three were joined in an Up-
bow slur:

This can be also be a handy device in the middle of a tune. I use it at the
close of the second bar in both the B- and E-parts of *The Kid On The
Mountain.* It means that the repeated phrase - bars 1 & 2 and 3 & 4 - can
be played with the same bowing each time.

---

57 THE KID ON THE MOUNTAIN

A great tune, full of variation. The first, third and fourth parts are in E minor, the second and fifth in G. Make the most of the contrast between the mellifluous third part with its high rolls and the staccato trebling effect of the section that follows. Tommy Peoples made a classic recording of this tune on his 1976 album with Paul Brady, *The High Part Of The Road* (Shanachie 29003), pairing it with another fine slip jig, *An Phis Fluich* or *O'Farrell's Welcome To Limerick*.

58 THE ROCKY ROAD TO DUBLIN

In the merry month of May from my home I started,
Left the girls of Tuam nearly broken-hearted,
Saluted father dear, kissed my darlin' mother,
Drank a pint of beer my grief and tears to smother,
Then off to reap the corn and leave where I was born,
I cut a stout blackthorn to banish ghost and goblin
In a brand new pair of brogues I rattled o'er the bogs
And frightened all the dogs on the Rocky Road to Dublin -
One, two, three, four, five - hunt the hare and turn her
Down the rocky road and all the ways to Dublin
　　　　Whack fol-lol de ra!

The song, for which a variant of this tune is used, tells of a Connachtman's adventures as
he travels to Dublin and then crosses the Irish Sea to Liverpool. Along the way he's robbed
and abused and the song ends with a grand fight in which "my shillelagh I let fly."

I'm reminded of another 19th century Irishman who travelled to England but, after a fight in
a bar, was obliged to leave again in a hurry and that was a piper, Patrick Walsh. According
to Francis O'Neill, he finally settled at Swineford, Co. Mayo "and taught his art to many
pupils who came from near and far for instruction on the pipes. His method of dismissing
his pupils was as unceremonious as his own departure from England. When one had
mastered a tune Walsh took the pupil's hat and flung it outdoors as a signal for the owner
to follow it."

In contrast to the last tune, each section of this slip-jig begins with an Up-bow - for no
better reason, I'm afraid, than that it feels more comfortable to me that way. Notice that
within the slurs the accent can fall on the first note, the end note or even the middle note of
three, according to context.

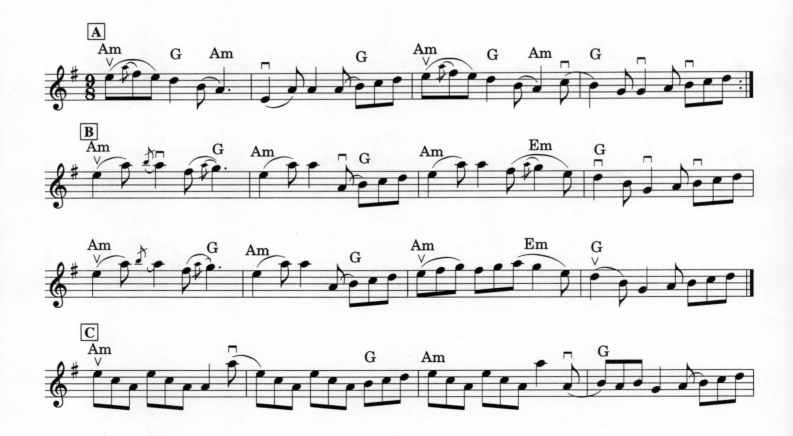

59 THE BUTTERFLY

This extraordinarily beautiful tune comes from Tommy Potts of Dublin, whose eccentric but brilliantly inventive approach to traditional music can be heard on the album *The Liffey Banks* (Claddagh CC13).

Tommy Potts   Photo: Jeffrey Craig, courtesy of Claddagh Records

JIGS 4

*I'm very haphazard. Like I don't play the same tune
in the same way twice - because I can't remember
how I played it the first time.*

Packie Manus Byrne, *Recollections of a Donegal Man*

Working through the tunes in this book, we have taken on board a wealth of bowing patterns and ornaments. Any tune can be played in a simpler or a more complex manner. Often it's what you <u>bring</u> to a tune, more than anything intrinsic to that particular melody, that makes it more or less of a challenge. And of course what seems tricky to one fiddle player may come very naturally to another. In the case of *Garrett Barry's,* for example, I give a simpler version followed by a more elaborate one; and personally I find the more elaborate version easier to play - but that's because it's a version that has evolved in my own playing over a period of years. Always keep in mind the basic <u>simplicity</u> of the music, the two-to-a-bar beat in the case of a jig, the melodic shape. Even if *The Chicago Jig* and *Tom Billy's* take hours of hard work to master, they should, in the end, sound easy, almost effortless.

Lots of rolls in this pair of tunes - second and third finger rolls as well as the open-string rolls we examined in *The Star Above The Garter.* The C-part of *The Chicago Jig* in particular is very densely ornamented. Take it slowly and be sure to avoid gripping the neck of the fiddle with your left hand. Bringing your left elbow well under the fiddle may help you reach across for those third-finger rolls on the D-string. Also make a point of emphasising the second main beat in each bar with a strong Up-bow to assist the forward movement of the tune and avoid getting bogged down.

60 THE CHICAGO JIG

Composed by Johnny Harling, a whistle player from Chicago, this fine three-part tune is also known as *The Dusty Windowsill.* The latter name was inspired, I am told, by the state of the windowsill in the men's toilets at the Irish Heritage Centre in downtown Chicago.

The device of playing **four notes in the space of a triplet** - which we looked at first in relation to *Tobin's Jig* - occurs in both the B and C-parts of *Tom Billy's*. The <u>lilt</u> with which the jig is played means that the first note of a triplet is longer than the others, so although what is written down here is two semiquavers (sixteenths) followed by two quavers (eighth notes), all four notes are of roughly equal length. Note that in bar B3 we use a Down bow to slur the two quavers at the end of the 'triplet'. In C4, in contrast, we use four short separate strokes. In both cases, the effect of the device is to introduce a temporary rhythmic disturbance that is very exciting.

61 TOM BILLY'S

Tom Billy Murphy (1879-1944) of Ballydesmond was Sliabh Luachra's most highly regarded fiddle player and teacher in the early part of the 20th century. Lame in one leg and blind, he was financially supported by his family. They owned a big house at Glencollins Upper, where he lived throughout his life. He travelled widely, by donkey, throughout the area to teach his fiddle pupils and was known as a character who, "with a wide knowledge of politics and world events...enjoyed sitting in pubs for hours on end arguing with people." (Alan Ward, *Music From Sliabh Luachra*). He is buried in Ballydesmond churchyard.

This version of the tune is based on the playing of Julia Clifford and Denis Murphy.

124

The first version of *Garrett Barry's* given here uses basic jig bowing and sparse ornamentation. The second includes more irregular slurs; the first two bars of the A-part are, when repeated, significantly altered; and the four-notes-into-three device, used on the repeat, also changes the character of the B-part. It's not a different tune, of course. But in several respects it feels different. I suppose it must be based on various versions I have listened to over the years, as well as reflecting my preferences and limitations as a fiddle player.

Whatever traditional musicians have at their disposal in the way of style and technique will be brought to bear on any tune they learn. That is why if you listen to a traditional tune played by a dozen different players you will quite possibly hear a dozen different versions. It's also why wide listening will enrich your own playing. A tune is not fixed. It is made up of variable elements and, having assimilated the components of a style, you will almost certainly begin, consciously or not, to construct your own version. The effect of 'the dots,' of course, is to pickle tunes - they remain preserved but lifeless. That is why it is essential to learn them by heart, to let them change and grow. Written music is used by traditional players just to jog the memory.

62 GARRETT BARRY'S

Garrett Barry was a great uilleann pipes player from West Clare, of the generation preceding Willie Clancy. Both this and the next tune are firm favourites with pipers. The chords indicated as D major or D minor would, incidentally, sound better played as 'open' chords, ie without the third (F# or F-natural) being included at all.

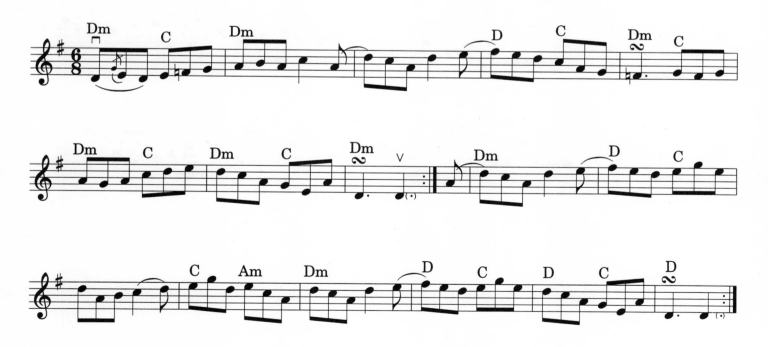

125

62A GARRETT BARRY'S

A more elaborate version of the same tune.

Although the Fs in the next tune are written as F#s it is not uncommon among some older Irish musicians for such notes to be flattened by about a quarter of a tone. (We have in fact come across half-sharps already - for example, in the single reel, *The Bank of Ireland*.) To the unaccustomed ear they might just sound plain out of tune, but *lonesome notes*, as Lucy Farr - my source for *The Pipe On The Hob* - calls them, are a subtle expressive resource. I once mentioned these half-sharp notes to Packie Byrne, the man quoted at the head of this chapter, and he knew exactly what I was referring to: "Ah," he says, "<u>blunt</u> notes!"

63 THE PIPE ON THE HOB

An archaic-sounding tune in the Mixolydian mode that I learned from Galway fiddle player Lucy Farr. It's a tune I also associate with Jimmy Power, originally from Ballyduff, Co. Waterford, another mainstay of the London Irish scene of the 1960s and 70s. He recorded it on his 1967 *Irish Dances* album. The image of a fiddle player sitting smoking by the fire, then maybe putting his pipe down on the hob while he plays a tune, brings to mind the opening of a song by West Clare fiddler Junior Crehan, recalling his mentor Scully Casey, the father of Bobby Casey:

> 'Tis often I rambled to Casey's
> And sat myself down on the hob
> And Scully'd be playing on the fiddle
> And the pipe in full steam in his gob.
> The smoke of his pipe and the music
> Up the chimney they'd go to the sky.
> May God rest your soul, Scully Casey,
> 'Tis a pity that you had to die.

MARCHES, WALTZES &
A SET DANCE TUNE

Part of the richness of the Irish musical tradition is the diversity of dance forms - and therefore different rhythms - that it encompasses. Reels, as we know, predominate, with jigs second and dance tunes of other types much fewer in number. In this section we'll examine some tunes that are all too easily overlooked but which can be handy additions to a fiddler's repertoire.

Marches

The march has four beats to the bar. These can be subdivided either into threes, as in the case of *Brian Boru's* (which is written here in 12/8 time), or into twos or fours, as in *Martin Kirwan's*. The pace is very steady and unhurried.

64 BRIAN BORU'S

"The harp was brought in and a blind young harper advanced who was, I was told, one of the most accomplished harpers in the neighbourhood; and in fact his music enraptured us all. The first piece he played was *Brian Boru's March*. The music of this march is wildly powerful and at the same time melancholy. It is at once the music of victory and of mourning. The rapid modulations and wild beauty of the airs was such that I think this march deserves fully to obtain a celebrity equal to that of the *Marseillaise* and the *Ragotsky*."

> - Kohl, German author of *Ireland* (1844) on his visit to a gentleman in Drogheda.

Brian Boru's popular reputation is of an Irish hero who fought to drive the Viking invaders out of Ireland. The story goes that after his heroic victory at Clontarf in 1014 he was treacherously murdered in his tent. Modern scholars believe that the army he defeated was in fact an alliance of Irishmen and vikings, the kings of Leinster having joined forces with the Dublin-based vikings to resist takeover by the O'Briens of Munster.

This version is based on that of *The Chieftains*, one of the most influential Irish bands of recent years.

65 MARTIN KIRWAN'S

Learned from Lucy Farr, a grand County Galway fiddle player whose father, Martin Kirwan, played it on the melodeon. It is very similar to a tune played by both Scottish and American Old Time musicians, *Campbell's Farewell To Red Castle* (or to *Red Gap*). The Scots version uses the so-called 'double tonic' - ie it is constructed on triads of G and F, instead of using the dominant chord of D, as we do here. Lucy Farr includes it on her cassette, *Heart and Home*.

Traditional musicians have always been in the habit of recycling old tunes to fit new rhythms. The set-dance *Rodney's Glory*, for instance, was based on an older air, *The Praises of Limerick*, and was in turn converted into both the reel *The Bank of Ireland* and the jig *Port Shean t Sheain*. With the introduction of the quadrille into Ireland around 1816 many old song airs were speeded up for dancing and the tradition lives on - as in the band *De Danann's* conversion of the Beatles song *Hey Jude* into a hornpipe. Belfast singer Freddy McKay even has a song about a 'Fenian record player' that 'speeded up *God Save The Queen* till it sounded like a jig!' Our first waltz, *The Star of the County Down*, started life as a well known song in common time and that version is given first.

66a STAR OF THE COUNTY DOWN

In Banbridge Town in the County Down
One morning last July
From a boreen green came a sweet colleen
And she smiled as she passed me by
She looked so sweet from her two bare feet
To the sheen of her nut brown hair
Such a coaxing elf sure I shook myself
To be sure I was really there.

From Bantry Bay up to Derry Quay
And from Galway to Dublin Town
No maid I've seen like the brown colleen
That I met in the County Down

A few years ago County Down's Gaelic football team had a very successful season and made it to the all-Ireland final. The slogan adopted by their supporters - 'Up Down!' - was widely heard, especially after the team won.

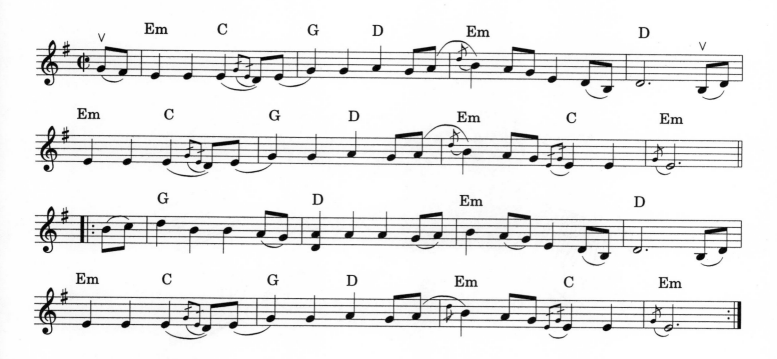

In Irish waltzes the tempo is always brisk - this is the country-style waltz, not the grand waltz of the Viennese ballroom.

66b STAR OF THE COUNTY DOWN
(Waltz)

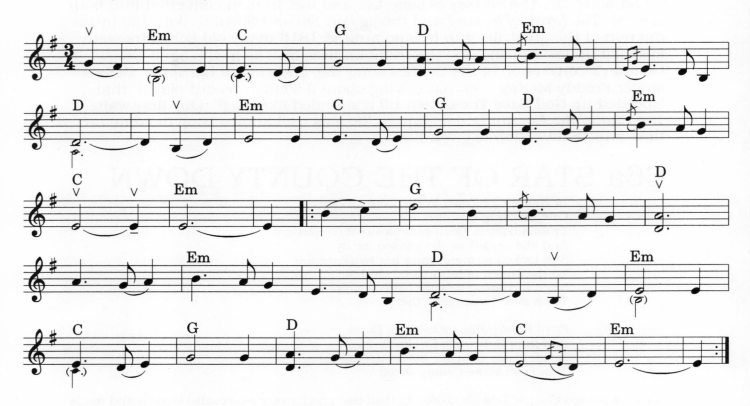

67 THE PALM TREES OF KERRY

O the palm trees wave on high
All around your fertile shore
Adieu, you hills of Kerry
I never shall see you more.
O why did I leave my home
And why did I cross the sea
And leave the small birds singing
Around you, sweet Tralee?

I learned this song in waltz-time from singer Peta Webb, who got it from traditional singer Sean Burke. After encountering widespread disbelief among English friends about the existence of such exotic vegetation in Ireland, Peta took her camera along and returned home with uncontestable proof!

Set dance tunes are simply those used for particular - 'set' - dances. There are several in common use, including *The Job of Journeywork, Rodney's Glory* and *The Garden of Daisies.* Don't confuse them with the dancing of *sets* - an abbreviation of *sets of quadrilles.* The example given here is similar to a hornpipe in its rhythm and tempo, but has a different number of bars - twelve to each section, rather than the usual eight.

68 ACE & DEUCE OF PIPERING

The title refers to the uilleann - pronounced *ill-yun* - pipes, a peculiarly Irish instrument that evolved from earlier types of bagpipes in the 18th century. The air bag is filled by means of a bellows and, in addition to a two-octave chanter on which the melody is played, the uilleann pipes also have drones and regulators for playing additional notes. *Pipering* is an old-fashioned term for piping. (I also like the old word for a flute-player or flautist - a *fluter*.) The title of this fine tune has been adopted by Na Piobairi Uilleann, the Dublin-based Irish Pipers' Society, for its annual concerts.

The Ace & Deuce of Piping

Wednesday 30th Sept. 1992 at 8pm

National Concert Hall

Jackie Daly – accordion
Catherine Ennis – organ
Seán Garvey – singer
Gay McKeon – uilleann pipes
Pádraic Mac Mathúna – uilleann pipes
Liam O'Flynn – uilleann pipes
Eoin Ó Riabhaigh – uilleann pipes
Paul O'Shaughnessy – fiddle
Desi Wilkinson – flute
The Crusheen Lancers Set
Brendan Kennelly – presenter
Brian Masterson – sound
Seán Potts – producer

Tickets £8, £10, £12 from National Concert Hall or
Na Píobairí Uilleann, 15 Henrietta St., Dublin 1, Tel. 730093

135

REELS 4

Then he asked me how many tunes did I think I played.
I told him I hadn't the least idea. 'Well,' says he, "I've been
keeping tab on you, and you have just played 436 reels,
not counting the others.'

- Timothy Dillon, fiddle player, quoted by Francis O'Neill.

In this section we'll look at ten more reels. We'll still be a few short of
Timothy Dillon's '436 reels, not counting the others' but, well - one step at
a time.

Figure of Eight Bowing

Look at bar A8 of the *Reel of Mullinavat*. The last two bow-strokes both
take us from a D on the A-string to an open E. (You could use a 4th finger
for the E but it would probably be less characteristic). As usual, the effect
of the triplet is to shift the accent to the off-beat, so that we have two
consecutive accents:

If those last two bow-strokes were repeated in a series it would become
apparent that your right wrist, as you look at it, is describing a **figure-of-
eight** on its side - or, if you prefer, the infinity symbol:

This kind of bowing is most effective if extra arm-weight is used at the
points in the diagram where the lines intersect - or, to put it another way,
on the note E. Insufficient weight can produce a false, glassy tone on the
open string - an annoying effect that can also be produced by a build-up of
rosin on the string. So let your elbow lead the bow confidently across.

---

69 THE REEL OF MULLINAVAT

The village of Mullinavat - in Irish, *Mull ar an Bhatta*, the Mill on the Sticks - is in Co. Kilkenny, about ten miles N.E. of Waterford. I went there on a musical pilgrimage in 1993 but no-one in the village seems to play traditional music these days; nor was anyone I spoke to aware of the village's fame among musicians. According to one resident, 'nothing of any significance has happened in Mullinavat for as long as anyone living here can remember.' Francis O'Neill, however, reporting the story of *Thady Connor (and How He Got His Pipes)* informs us that "Well, Thady's pipes were old and cracked and had a squeak in 'em that bate the Mullinavat pig all hollow." So the village does seem to have had at least one famous resident! I learned the tune from the playing of the great New York fiddle player, Andy McGann.

Consecutive Rolls

In bar A1 of the next tune we have two first-finger rolls, a *short* roll and a *long* roll, both on the same principal note, B. As you can see when they're written out in full, the only difference between them is the placing of the accent:

In the first case it precedes the roll, in the second it follows. In both cases, though, it falls on the off-beat. Try the bowing pattern - minus the notes:

It may help to listen to the Learning Disc. Practice at half-speed or less while you're sorting out - both in your mind and on the fiddle - the relationship between the notes. Then, gradually, speed up. Consecutive rolls also occur as a variant of bar A3 of *The Jug of Punch* and in the B-part of *Eddie Kelly's* reel.

70 DOCTOR GILBERT

Another of the classic E minor Irish reels, I learned this one too from the playing of Andy McGann, who calls it *Dr Gilbert's Fancy Concert Reel.* Donegal fiddler John Doherty called it *The Dispute At The Crossroads*, in reference to an argument between the police and his uncle, Mickey McConnell, whose spirited performance of the tune (as he was walking home from a dance in the early hours of the morning!) drew their attention to the state he was in.

The next pair of tunes also make a fine set. Don't be surprised if it takes a long time before they come easily. Like many Irish reels, they are fairly challenging, particularly perhaps the crossing from the D- to the E-string in the B-part of *Paddy Ryan's Dream*. You may find it helpful to play tunes without the rolls, concentrating at first on the melodic outline - and don't rush!

Michael Coleman
1891-1991

A
Centenary
Celebration
of the
works of
Michael
Coleman

71 LAD O'BEIRNE'S

James "Lad" O'Beirne was the son of Philip O'Beirne who had taught the young Michael Coleman, back in Sligo. When Lad arrived in New York as a teenager in 1928 somebody took him along to meet the now famous Coleman. They played some tunes together and then Coleman was told "This is Phil O'Beirne's son, Lad." He was so moved by the memory of his former teacher that he put down his fiddle and wept. He and Lad O'Beirne became close friends and associates. (This story of their meeting is from Harry Bradshaw's book about Coleman).

Variant A5   Variant B1 + B2

72 PADDY RYAN'S DREAM

Recorded by Coleman in 1921, this tune is also known as *Miss Lyle's Reel* and, in Scotland, as *The Reel Of Tulloch*. In her notes to the 1976 *Kathleen Collins* album (Shanachie 29002) Jean Stewart refers in passing to "Paddy Ryan the Roscommon fiddler" but I know no more about him than that.

140

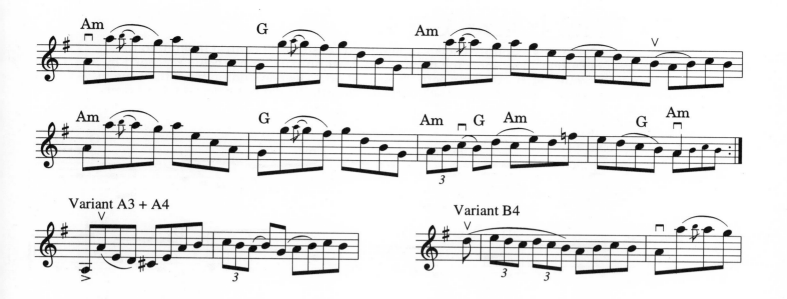

Variant A3 + A4

Variant B4

Paddy Ryan's Dream is one of the few tunes we have learned so far to make use of the fiddle's fourth string. The lowest note on the uilleann pipes is D (corresponding to our open D-string), so any tune that goes lower than that excludes pipers, thus perhaps limiting its chances of survival. Still, the warm, dark tone of the fiddle G-string is worth exploring, as the next two pairs of reels also demonstrate.

73 WALSH'S FANCY

Both this reel and the next were learned from the playing of County Galway fiddle player, the late Aggie Whyte. The third- and second-finger rolls in A4 are not easy - be patient and take it slowly.

74 THE LADS OF LAOIS

A tune full of yearning. County Laois - pronounced *Leesh* - is in central Ireland, to the south west of Dublin. The short roll in bar A7 is most unusual in not being preceded by a quaver of the same pitch - this one actually <u>feels</u> short. The descending bit of the tune in bars B5 and B6 is so delicious I usually alternate it with the variant below, to avoid over-using it.

75 THE JUG OF PUNCH

Both this and *Eddie Kelly's* were learned from the playing of Kathleen Collins. She got them from Paddy Fahy, fiddle player and composer from Kilconnel, County Galway and one-time member of the Aughrim Slopes Ceilidh Band. (And of whom, more later). Like many of the South Galway tunes, this one has a plaintive, modal quality. It shares its title, if nothing else, with a fine old drinking song:

> What more pleasure could a boy desire
> Than to sit him down-o beside the fire
> And in his hand-o a jug of punch
> Aye, and on his knee-o a tidy wench.

76 EDDIE KELLY'S

Eddie Kelly is a living composer of fiddle tunes, some of them very original in manner. Notice how the usual pattern of two-bar phrases - a fairly evenly balanced question and response - is disrupted here, the first phrase running on for three bars as far as the F (the dotted crotchet) in A3 and being answered rather curtly in A4.

While some reels are undoubtedly more difficult than others, much of the apparent complexity in a fiddler's rendition of a tune is, as I said earlier, a matter of what he or she brings to it in the way of technical expertise. The next pair of reels <u>can</u> be among the most elaborately varied and ornamented reels in the entire Irish fiddle repertoire. The versions here, however, are fairly straightforward. I'll leave it up to you to hunt out other ways of playing them. Wide listening and close attention to other musicians, not necessarily just fiddle players, will open your ears to what's possible. And then there's your own ingenuity too...

77 BONNIE KATE

'*Bonnie Kate*, a particular favourite among fiddle players because of the highly decorative setting in which the Sligo fiddle player, Michael Coleman, played it, was composed by Daniel Dow, a fiddler from Perthshire. It was first published around 1760 under the name of *The Bonnie Lass of Fisherrow*.' - Breandan Breathnach, *Folk Music & Dances Of Ireland*.

The piper Seamus Ennis had a story involving this tune that was told by Sliabh Luachra fiddle player Padraig O'Keefe: "I was in the front bar," Padraig says, "and in came these people - two men and a woman. And they said, 'Padraig, will you play a tune and she'll dance to it.' And I got the fiddle and started in with a reel - *Bonnie Kate*. And then suddenly there was a raid. It was after hours. The Gards in. And I was playing away engrossed with *Bonnie Kate* and the girl dancing and I wasn't watching out. I played away with my backside to the counter. 'What's your name?' - the Gards. And she had gone, the dancer, all scattered, all gone like that. And there was I with my backside to the counter, flogging *Bonnie Kate*. Seven-and-sixpence *Bonnie Kate* cost me!"
- Quoted by Alan Ward, *Music From Sliabh Luachra*.

Padraig O'Keefe, late 1950s

78 JENNY'S CHICKENS

Associated with *Bonnie Kate* ever since Coleman's recording of the two tunes, this is an intense-sounding single reel, similar to *The Morning Dew*, though in the Dorian mode of B. It is thought Coleman may have adapted it from the Scottish reel *Sleepy Maggy*. The title of this tune reminds me of something that Rose, an elderly Irish neighbour of mine, says if ever we've been talking about hard times: 'Ah well,' she says. 'To Hell with poverty, we'll kill a chicken.'

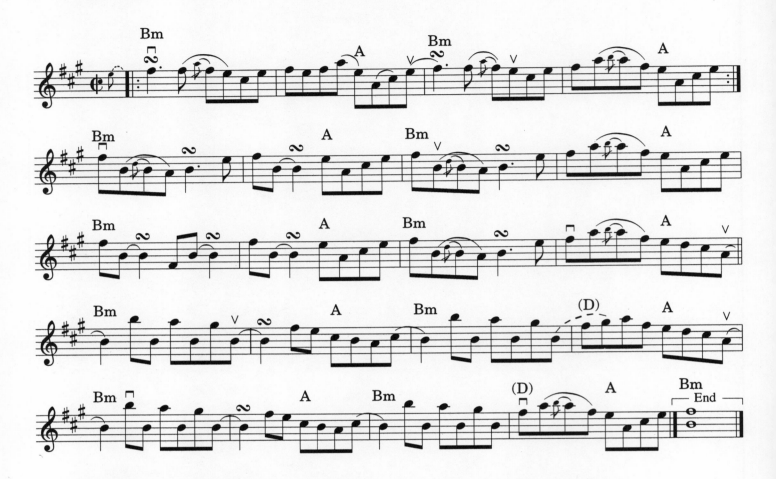

Denis Murphy   *Courtesy of Topic Records*

John Docherty

ANOTHER REEL, ANOTHER JIG

There is only one way of becoming a traditional singer or player,
and that is by listening to genuine material played in a traditional manner.

- Breandan Breathnach, *Folk Music And Dances of Ireland*

The following short history shows how a new tune can enter the tradition. The next (and final) reel in this book was composed by Paddy Fahy, of Kilconnel, County Galway. Lucy Farr, a fellow County Galway fiddle player who in the mid-1980s was living in London but still paid visits 'back home', learned it from Paddy at a session in Loughrea. She in turn passed it on to me and I taught it to some of my students in London. In 1993 a friend sent me a tape, *Came The Dawn,* by fiddle player Seamus Creagh, recorded in Newfoundland, Canada and including this same reel, now, to my surprise, entitled *Pete Cooper's.* Seamus says he learned it 'from a tape of Pete Cooper, a fiddle player from London.' Exactly what tape that could have been is still a mystery to me, but no matter, it's a gem of a reel. Lucy herself has now recorded it on her cassette album *Heart And Home* and I pass it on to you, not exactly as Seamus plays it, nor quite as Lucy plays it, but as I've got used to it myself. I've no doubt that if I hear *your* version in a few years' time it'll be a little different again, because none of us, thanks be to God, are ever really in charge of what happens with traditional music.

79 PADDY FAHY'S *(Pete Cooper's!)*
Remember that in the South Galway style the F#s are played 'blunt.'

Let me give you one last tune, again passed on to me by Lucy Farr, again recorded on *Heart And Home*. Paddy Fahy composed it, I believe, in the mid-1980s and, as Lucy pointed out, it's really a jig-time version of the reel we just learned. Whether or not either of these last tunes can yet be said to have 'entered the tradition' is difficult to say. Both are certainly known, accepted and enjoyed by certain groups of players in certain places. Only time will tell how widely they spread from their original source.

80 ANOTHER ONE OF PADDY'S

'Paddy does come out with some rare stuff. It's music from the soul. I'll play you another one of Paddy's jigs I got from him last year. It's a new one.'

- Lucy Farr at a fiddle workshop, October 1986

Seamus Creagh, Cork, October 1993   *Photo: Marie-Anniek Desplanques*

We have ended, as we began, with an easy jig. Thanks for joining me on this excursion into the world of Irish fiddle music. It can, as we have discovered, be fiercely complicated stuff. And it can also be very simple. Keep listening to as much traditional music as you can, both live and recorded. If you go along to sessions and concerts certain tunes will probably detach themselves from the musical multitude and leap out at you, demanding to be learned, so just follow your inclination. As for style and technique, you will always find more to learn because, as long as the music is alive and changing, there will in fact never be such a thing as a 'complete' Irish fiddle player. Enjoy yourself.

Some useful addresses

For information on music festivals and other places to hear live traditional music, contact:

Comhaltas Ceoltoiri Eireann, 32 Belgrave Square, Monkstown,
Co. Dublin - Telephone 01-280 0295
(The association also has other branches in Ireland as well as abroad).

Na Piobairi Uilleann (The Uilleann Pipers Society), 15 Henrietta St.
Dublin 1 - Telephone 01-873 0093

An outstanding collection of books and recordings etc of the music is kept at the:
Irish Traditional Music Archive, 63 Merrion Square, Dublin 2
Telephone 01-661 9699 fax 01-668 6260

The author and fiddle, London 1994   Photo: Ivan Coleman

Recommended Listening

This is not a full discography of Irish fiddle music but a personal selection that I hope will be at least a starting point. Some of the albums are only on cassette. I make a rough division between what I think of as more purely traditional recordings, generally by older - or deceased - players (list A) and those by younger present-day performers, including bands (list B).

List A

Vincent Campbell, Francie Byrne, Con Cassidy & James Byrne
The Brass Fiddle - Claddagh Records CC44 (LP) 4CC44 (cassette)

Bobby Casey
Casey In The Cowhouse - Bellbridge Records 001

Julia Clifford & Denis Murphy
The Star Above The Garter - Claddagh Records, CC5CD

Padraig O'Keefe, Denis Murphy & Julia Clifford
Kerry Fiddles - Topic Records TCSCD 309

Michael Coleman
Michael Coleman 1891-1945 - Viva Voce /Gael Linn, CEF 161

John Doherty
Bundle And Go - (USA) Green Linnet GLCD 3077 / (Europe) Ossian OSS 17

Mickey Doherty
The Gravel Walks - Comhairle Bhealoideas Eireann CBE 002

Lucy Farr
Heart And Home - Veteran Tapes VT123

Vincent Griffin
Vincent Griffin - Ossian OSS 73

Paddy Killoran
Paddy Killoran's Back In Town - Shanachie SH33003

Sean MacGuire
Sean MacGuire & Joe Burke - COXCD 015

Sean MacNamara, Eamonn Coyne & Peggy Peakin
The Long Strand - Veteran Tapes VT125

James Morrison
The Professor - Viva Voce 001

Rose Murphy
Milltown Lass - Ossian OSS21

Tommy Potts	*The Liffey Banks* - Claddagh Records CC13
Jimmy Power	*Irish Fiddle* - Ossian OSS 81
Various - including Mairtin Byrnes, Bobby Casey, Jimmy Power etc	*Paddy In The Smoke* - Ossian OSS 19

List B

Altan	*Horse With A Heart* - Green Linnet GL1078 *Angel Island* - Green Linnet GLCD1137
The Bothy Band	*The First Album, 1975* - (USA) Green Linnet GL3011/(Europe) Mulligan LUNCD 002 *The Best Of The Bothy Band* - (USA) Green Linnet GL3001/(Europe) Mulligan LUNCD 041
Kevin Burke	*Up Close* - Green Linnet GLCD 1052 *If The Cap Fits* - (USA) Green Linnet GL3009/(Europe) Mulligan LUNCD 021
Patrick Street (featuring Kevin Burke)	*Patrick Street* - Green Linnet GL1071
James Byrne	*The Road To Glenlough* - Claddagh Records CC52 (LP) 4CC52 (cassette)
Liz Carroll	*Liz Carroll* - Green Linnet GLCD 1092
Nollaig Casey & Arty McGlynn	*Lead The Knave* - Round Tower MCG1
The Chieftains	*The Chieftains* - Claddagh Records CC2CD also *The Chieftains 2, 3, 4, 5* etc etc, all on Claddagh
Kathleen Collins	*Kathleen Collins* - Shanachie SH29002
Pete Cooper	*The Wounded Hussar* - Fiddling From Scratch FFSCD 002
Matt Cranitch	*Eistigh Seal* - Gael Linn CEF 104 *Take A Bow* - Ossian OSSCD 5
Seamus Creagh	*Came The Dawn* - Ossian OSSCD 90

De Danann	*Anthem* - Dara DARACD 013
	Ballroom - Green Linnet GL3040
Frankie Gavin	*Frankie Goes To Town* - Bee's Knees BKCD 001 /(USA) Green Linnet GL3051
Frankie Gavin & Paul Brock	*A Tribute To Joe Cooley* - Gael Linn CEF 115
Paddy Glackin	*Paddy Glackin* - Gael Linn CEFC 060
	In Full Spate - Gael-Linn CEF CD 153
Martin Hayes	*Martin Hayes* - Green Linnet GLCD 1127
Sean Keane	*Jig It In Style* - Claddagh CCF25CD
Andy McGann (with Paul Brady)	*It's A Hard Road To Travel* - Shanachie SH29009
Tommy Peoples	*The High Part Of The Road* (with Paul Brady) Shanachie SH29003
	The Iron Man (with Daithi Sproule) - Shanachie SH79044
	Matt Molloy, Paul Brady, Tommy Peoples - Mulligan LUNCD 017
Stockton's Wing	*The Collection* - Tara TARA4

Pete Cooper - **THE WOUNDED HUSSAR** *Fiddling From Scratch* **CDFFS 002/ FFS 002** (tape) *Irish fiddle music with:* Kathryn Locke *cello* - Steafan Hannigan *bodhran & uilleann pipes* - Luke Daniels *button accordion* - Tina Johansson *percussion* - Lawrie Wright *guitar & double bass* - Geoff Coombs *mandola & mandolin* - Jenny Newman *viola*

1 The Reel of Mullinavat / Doctor Gilbert
2 The Chicago Jig / Tom Billy's
3 Julia Clifford's Polka / Din Tarrant's
4 O'Carolan's Draught
5 Garrett Barry's / Pipes on the Hob
6 Donegal Mazurkas
7 The Jug of Punch / Eddie Kelly's
8 The Wounded Hussar
9 Toormore / The Cullen Slide
10 Musical Priest / Salamanca / Morning Dew / The Heart Is True
11 Ace & Deuce of Pipering
12 Donegal Highlands
13 Bryan O'Lynn / The Connachtman's Rambles / Paddy Clancy's
14 Lad O'Beirne's / Paddy Ryan's Dream
15 McGlinchey's Hornpipe

'A mighty collection of Irish music performed... with a freshness and flowing ease of delivery that is the mark of a supreme practitioner'- *Rock'n'Reel*
'Flawless, authentic-sounding fiddle playing from a master...the sound he makes is wholly evocative of the best of the old-time fiddlers' - John Paddy Browne, *Folk On Tap*
'A truly delightful collection of Irish fiddle music played with love, understanding and soul...beautifully recorded and presented'- Dave Arthur, *English Dance And Song*

Available from: **Claddagh Records Music Shop**, 2 Cecilia Street, Dublin 2, Ireland. Tel 01-677 0262 **Andy's Front Hall**, PO Box 307, Wormer Road, Voorheesville, NY 12186, USA. Tel 518-765 4193 **Topic Records,** 50 Stroud Green Road, London, N4 3EF, UK. Tel 0171-263 6403/1240

Also by Pete Cooper - ALL AROUND THE WORLD *Fiddling From Scratch* (Tape only) **FFS 001** *Fiddle Music from Ireland, Scandinavia, Eastern Europe and the USA with* Lawrie Wright *guitar* - Paulette Gershen *whistle* - Mark Emerson *fiddle* - Holly Tannen *Appalachian dulcimer* - Candy Goldman *5-string banjo* - Sandy Silva *feet* - Kathryn Locke *cello* & Geoff Coombs *mandola, bodhran*

Side A	**Side B**
1 Maggie Pickens/	1 Little Rabbit
Molly Will You Marry Me?	2 Lucy Farr's Polkas
2 Swallow's Tail (reel)	3 The Chancellor/Galway Bay (hornpipes)
3 Norwegian Reinlender	4 Norwegian Bridal March
4 Ducks On The Pond	5 Three Rucenitsas (Bulgarian)
5 Yellow Rose Of Texas	6 Waltz From Vårmland
6 Hungarian Songs	7 Bessarabian Wedding Dance
7 All Around The World/Butter-	8 The Arkansas Traveller
milk Mary/Fergal O'Gara/	
Green Fields of Ross Beigh	
8 The Blarney Pilgrim (Jig)	

'In lesser musicians there often seems to be a trade-off between virtuosity & soul, with technique developing at the expense of passion. Not so with Cooper who supplies both in large measure...The quality never drops below the very highest level' - Andy Cheyne, *Folk Roots*. A booklet - also called *All Around The World* - of all the tunes on the tape is available from Dragonfly Music, 10 Gibson Street, Newbiggin-by-the-Sea, Northumberland, NE64 6PE, UK. Tel 0670-818540

Tunes in Alphabetical Order